3rd
EDITION

The *Paraprofessional's Guide*
to the *Inclusive Classroom*

3rd EDITION

The *Paraprofessional's Guide* to the *Inclusive Classroom*

Working as a Team

 by

Mary Beth Doyle, Ph.D.

Saint Michael's College
Colchester, Vermont

·P A U L·H·
BROOKES
PUBLISHING Co.®

Baltimore • London • Sydney

Paul H. Brookes Publishing Co.
Post Office Box 10624
Baltimore, Maryland 21285-0624
USA

www.brookespublishing.com

"Paul H. Brookes Publishing Co." is a registered trademark of
Paul H. Brookes Publishing Co., Inc.

Manufactured in the United States of America by
Versa Press, Inc., East Peoria, Illinois.

The case studies in this book are composites based on the authors' experiences. In most instances, names and identifying details have been changed to protect confidentiality. In other cases, individual names and stories are used by permission.

The photographs that appear on the cover and throughout this book are used by permission of the individuals pictured or by their parents or guardians.

Purchasers of *The Paraprofessional's Guide to the Inclusive Classroom: Working as a Team, Third Edition,* are granted permission to photocopy the individual forms in this volume for distribution for educational purposes. None of the forms may be reproduced to generate revenue for any program or individual. Photocopies may only be made from an original book. *Unauthorized use beyond this privilege is prosecutable under federal law.* You will see the copyright protection notice at the bottom of each photocopiable page.

Cover photograph by Jerry Swope.

Library of Congress Cataloging-in-Publication Data

Doyle, Mary Beth.
   The paraprofessional's guide to the inclusive classroom: Working as a team / by Mary Beth Doyle.—3rd ed.
      p.   cm.
   Includes index.
   ISBN-13: 978-1-55766-924-7
   ISBN-10: 1-55766-924-4
   1. Inclusive education—United States.   2. Teachers' assistants—United States.   3. Teaching
   teams—United States.   I. Title.
   LC1201.D69 2008
   371.9'046—dc22   2007051171

British Library Cataloguing in Publication data are available from the British Library.

2012   2011

10   9   8   7   6   5   4   3   2

Contents

About the Author.. vii

How to Use This Book ix

What's New in This Edition? xi

Acknowledgments.. xiii

1   The Paraprofessional: Changing Roles and Responsibilities 1

     Where Do Teams Begin?
     What Is Inclusion?
     Who Are Paraprofessionals?
     What Are the Paraprofessional's Responsibilities in an Inclusion-Oriented
       Classroom?
     What Training and Support Do Paraprofessionals Require?
     Activity 1: Basic Role Differentiation
     Activity 2: Activity Debriefing
     Activity 3: Role Clarification with a Twist
     Application and Review of the Law

2   The Inclusive Classroom: Being a Member of the Team 19

     Activity 4: What Is a Team?
     Who Am I Working With?
     Who Is Responsible for What?
     What Is My Daily Schedule?
     Activities 5 and 6: Developing and Discussing the Paraprofessional's Daily Schedule
     Up-Front Issues to Reach Consensus On
     Effects of Paraprofessional Proximity
     Self-Advocates' Perspectives on Paraprofessional Proximity
     Team Member Communication

3   Supporting Individual Students 39

     How Do We Include Families in Educational Planning?
     Who Is the Student?
     Why Is Classroom Participation Important?
     What Is an Individualized Education Program?
     How Does the Paraprofessional Use an Individualized Education Program?

Why Are Student Schedules Important?
Activity 7: Who Is Peter?

4   Providing Curricular and Individualized Instructional Support 53

What Are Our Team's Expectations for Students?
What Are Our Team's Role Expectations?
Characteristics of Effective Paraprofessional Support
What Are Multilevel Curriculum and Instruction and Curriculum Overlapping?
What Are Learning Outcomes and General Supports?
Activity 8: Categorizing Goals and Objectives
How Do We Organize Curriculum Priorities Through Deliberate
    Communication?
How Can We Arrange the Classroom Routine to Support Diverse Learners?
How Does Unit Planning Support Diverse Learners?
What Is Preteaching?
What Are the Common Components of Daily Routines?
What Is Partial Participation?
How Are Instructional Prompts Provided?
How Are Curricular Adaptations Used?
What Is Delayed Responding?
How Can Note-Taking Strategies Support a Variety of Students?
Putting It All Together

5   Encouraging Positive Behaviors 87

What Are the Five Tenets of Positive Behavioral Support?
Activity 9: Positive Statements About Kids
Activity 10: Creating a Positive Atmosphere
What Are the Five Purposes of Behaviors?
Activity 11: Attention Seeking
How Should We Address Challenging Behaviors?
How Do We Design a Positive Behavior Support Plan?
How Do We Implement a Positive Behavior Support Plan?

6   Maintaining Confidentiality 111

Specialized Instruction
Remembering the Goals of Many Students
Maintaining Confidentiality
Activity 12: A Situation You Know About

References 119
Resources 123
Appendix A   Activities 125
Appendix B   Para Forms 135
Index 169

About the Author

Mary Beth Doyle, Ph.D., Associate Professor of Education, Saint Michael's College, 1 Winooski Park, Colchester, VT 05439

Mary Beth's primary work is in teacher preparation. She supports undergraduate and graduate students who are seeking initial licensure in secondary education or in special education. In this capacity she has the opportunity to encourage her students to develop the knowledge, skills, and dispositions necessary to create classroom communities where all students are welcomed, valued, and included. Mary Beth's interests include paraprofessional training and support, curriculum adaptations and accommodations, and collaboration. Mary Beth's writing and training activities focus on creating positive learning communities where all students are supported by a variety of adults.

How to Use This Book

The purpose of *The Paraprofessional's Guide to the Inclusive Classroom: Working as a Team, Third Edition,* is to provide introductory information that is needed for the paraprofessional, the general educator, and the special educator to better understand one another's roles and responsibilities in the inclusive classroom. This book is not meant to be a "how-to guide" for paraprofessionals. Rather, the goal is for the team to work through the chapters together so that as a team, you can create a shared understanding of the instructional context and process. Such an understanding will build a stronger, more effective instructional team.

This book also provides specific instruction related to students with disabilities in inclusive classrooms. In order to participate in the activities and discussions presented in this manual, it is strongly recommended that every member of the education team commit to engaging in the activities and readings together. Completing all of the activities should take approximately 5 hours of training time. Training can be structured according to team availability and preference (e.g., one full in-service day, five 1-hour blocks of time).

Keep in mind that a paraprofessional's role necessitates that he or she work with certified educators or other certified team members to apply the information contained in this book in the most appropriate manner. It would be inappropriate for the team to expect the paraprofessional to read and apply this information in isolation.

What's New in This Edition?

There are many elements of this third edition that are different from the previous editions. The anecdotes, interviews, and examples have been updated, and many forms have been edited based on feedback from teachers. However, the most significant difference is the increased emphasis on paraprofessionals' voices. There is a new topic strand that is present throughout the text that is referred to as Paraprofessional Self-Advocacy.

The Paraprofessional Self-Advocacy sections have been created to assist paraprofessionals in asking questions related to specific content areas. The questions are worded in a way to function as reminders to the classroom teachers and special educators, ensuring that they are giving the paraprofessionals the direction and support that is required by law.

This edition also offers self-reflection opportunities for all members of the team. The Paraprofessional Self-Reflection sections are meant to give paraprofessionals an opportunity to think about how these new elements of learning connect with both the immediate work and, in a broader sense, how we move toward creating communities where all members belong and are celebrated for their gifts.

This edition also offers a balance of middle and secondary applications and examples, as well as the traditional elementary examples. Now there are enough examples at each level to better support elementary, middle, and high school teams.

Acknowledgments

I would like to express my gratitude to the many classroom teachers and paraprofessionals who continue to challenge and encourage me to problem-solve through the important issues related to creating classroom communities.

A special thanks goes to the Cunningham family for their contributions to this edition. Your vision offered me such clarity and connection. Thank you.

Thank you to Saint Michael's College photojournalist Jerry Swope for his photo contributions. You captured the heart and soul of friendship.

I want to thank the Paul H. Brookes Publishing Co. staff, who continue to do the important work of designing and producing works that improve the lives of members of our communities. A special thanks to Marie Abate, for her amazing attention to details. Thank you, Rebecca Lazo, for the gentle encouragement and "can do" attitude that kept this project moving forward.

To my own students from Saint Michael's College in Vermont, who continue to inspire me with their courage and determination to become excellent teachers for all students who enter their classes: I wish each of you good energy and clear vision.

To Andrew Whiteford,
my longtime friend and teacher:
Andrew, you are one of those amazing people
who continues to add goodness to all who know you.

And to Noelle:
You have added so much joy into my life, and I thank you.

1

The Paraprofessional
Changing Roles and Responsibilities

Objectives

- Describe the characteristics of an *inclusive classroom*
- Define *paraprofessional*
- Describe the paraprofessional's roles and responsibilities
- Differentiate between the responsibilities of general educators, special educators, and paraprofessionals
- Explain the training and support paraprofessionals require
- Demonstrate paraprofessional self-advocacy skills

Did you know that the position of paraprofessional continues to be one of the fastest growing positions in public education? In the early 1960s, approximately 10,000 paraprofessionals were working in schools, primarily in noninstructional capacities (Green & Barnes, 1989). When the first edition of this book was published in 1997, estimates were unreliable, as there were no standardized reporting procedures. At that time, estimates of the numbers of paraprofessionals employed in public schools across the United States were between 300,000 and 500,000 (Giangreco, Edelman, Broer, & Doyle, 2001; Logue, 1993; U.S. Department of Education, 1993). Years later, there are still no standardized systems of reporting such data, although estimates have increased significantly (Pickett, Likins, & Wallace, 2003). In 1999, the U.S. Department of Education estimated that there were 621,000 instructional aides working in schools in the 1999–2000 school year; other sources suggested that the number was closer to 1 million paraprofessionals (Pickett et al., 2003). The National Center for Educational Statistics reported that as of 2003, U.S. schools employed 685,242 paraprofessionals (Snyder, Tan, & Hoffman, 2006). Employment projections indicate that this number will continue to grow.

The exact number of paraprofessionals is not the primary issue here. Rather, the issues are as follows:

1. Minimally, there is agreement that the number of paraprofessionals working in public schools continues to grow at a steady pace, yet no single agency is responsible for tracking related statistics.

2. There is increased attention to paraprofessionals' roles and responsibilities.

3. The use of paraprofessionals continues to increase despite the lack of research regarding its relationship to improved student outcomes.

4. In many situations, overreliance on paraprofessionals has resulted in students with the most challenging learning characteristics being taught by personnel with the least amount of training or expertise and students without disabilities or with high-incidence disabilities being taught by highly qualified, certified teachers.

Increasingly, students with disabilities are receiving their education in general education classrooms, and these classrooms are much more diverse than ever. General education classrooms encompass students from all races, countries, and socioeconomic classes. As the diversity of classrooms expands and deepens and students with disabilities are welcomed into these classrooms, new, interesting, and at times challenging opportunities arise. These challenges are often related to additional responsibilities, demands, and expectations encountered by general education teachers. One response to the challenges of increased diversity has been to hire paraprofessionals to assist teachers in meeting the new demands of including students with disabilities in the general education classroom. Unfortunately, in some cases this has become a reactive response rather than a systematic and proactive plan (Giangreco, Broer, & Edelman, 2002; Giangreco, Suter, & Doyle, in press). Schools rarely examine students' support needs prior to hiring individual, untrained paraprofessionals to assist with the education of students who experience the most significant learning challenges (Giangreco et al., 2002).

Although exploring this systems issue is beyond the scope of this text, you are encouraged to access *Schoolwide Planning to Improve Paraeducator Supports* (Giangreco, Edelman, & Broer, 2003) if your school is prepared for such work. A comprehensive annotated bibliography of research, planning, and training resources can be found at http://www.uvm .edu/~cdci/parasupport.

Whether or not entire schools decide to take on the issues related to supporting paraprofessionals, your individual team can make a significant difference in this area. Begin by asking the following questions when you are trying to decide if paraprofessional support is the type of assistance your team needs in order to support the diversity within your classroom.

- What are the learning and support needs of the students in this classroom?

- What are the most logical and necessary instructional interventions?

- Do the management and instructional needs of this heterogeneous classroom call for a trained person (e.g., special educator, related services provider) or an untrained person (e.g., paraprofessional) to assist the classroom teacher?

- If you believe that paraprofessional support would best meet your team's needs, specifically what would the paraprofessional do?

Although general education classrooms have changed significantly since the 1970s (and not just in relationship to welcoming students with disabilities), the basic operation of classrooms remains the same. Generally, one teacher is responsible for 25–35 students who have a variety of strengths and needs, represent many different cultures, speak many languages, and have had many different experiences outside of the classroom. Teachers are responsible for teaching all of these students, meeting standards, and being certain that all students pass a variety of standardized tests. Clearly, the pressures on classroom teachers are extraordinary, and in many cases the expectations placed on them are unreasonable given their daily working conditions (e.g., large class sizes, limited budgets, limited planning time, inadequate support from administration, limited opportunity for collaboration, weeks of testing that take away from instructional time). The information in this book is intended to offer relief for teachers, special educators, and paraprofessionals on very practical levels by assisting teams to improve communication and planning.

As classroom teachers are being required to do increasingly complex tasks, so too are paraprofessionals. Paraprofessionals are being asked to assist with everything from creating classroom and school communities in which all students are welcomed and supported to providing supplemental and, in far too many cases, initial instruction (Chopra & French, 2004; French, 2001; Riggs & Mueller, 2001).

WHERE DO TEAMS BEGIN?

Perhaps the best place to start change is with an examination of your school and classroom cultures. A sense of community that includes all members (i.e., adults and students) is a necessary aspect of every healthy school. Students, faculty, and staff are more likely to be more supportive of each other when there is a palpable sense of ease, belonging, and safety. To evaluate the climate in your own school, first examine the experiences of the adults in the school and then look at those of the students.

Here are several questions to consider as you begin to take the pulse of your school. Do you yourself feel safe? Are you welcomed? Do people greet you with kindness? Next, look at teachers and paraprofessionals who are around you and try to imagine their daily experiences. Do they experience the school as a positive and inclusive workplace? Notice how often you hear others address the paraprofessionals by their names, invite them to lunch in the faculty/staff room, and thank them for the work they do. What would it take to invite them into the center of the professional community, where they would be valued for their contributions?

Now, think about the students with disabilities in your school. What are their names? Who knows and interacts with them during formal (e.g., classes) and informal (e.g., cafeteria, recess) times? Are they visible and involved in classes? Do general education teachers include them in meaningful ways during instruction? Is it common to see students with and without disabilities talking, playing, and being together and helping one another on projects? Do students with disabilities spend more time with adults than with their peers? Does a paraprofessional sit with them in class and in the cafeteria? Do the students with disabilities enter the school at the same time as their peers, through the same doors?

To help in this assessment, invite several teachers and paraprofessionals to complete Para Form 1: Community Self-Assessment Checklist, located in the Para Forms appendix. After each person is finished, sit together at lunch or after school to answer these questions: 1) Where are our strengths and needs? 2) What will we prioritize for change this year? 3) How will we measure progress toward our goal(s) of building community? It is important that this conversation be facilitated with a sense of positive energy and a belief that, though things may not be perfect in your classroom or school community, there certainly are strengths to build on. Most teachers have an intuitive sense of optimism; this is a time to apply that optimism!

WHAT IS INCLUSION?

At its root, inclusion is a value upon which decisions are based, a value that holds that all members of the school community are important and necessary for the community's success. The collective ability of those in the community to move from the ideal of inclusion to its reality is where opportunities and challenges emerge. The time is right for everyone to work together to create communities in which all children and youth are welcomed. Imagine the impact this could have on the world!

To be considered inclusive, a classroom or school must exhibit each of the following characteristics (Giangreco, Baumgart, & Doyle, 1995; York-Barr, Kronberg, & Doyle, 1996):

- All students with disabilities are accepted and welcomed unconditionally in their local community school.

- Students with disabilities are valued members of the school community, as are their neighbors and siblings without disabilities.

- Students with disabilities are placed in grades and classes on the basis of chronological age.

- Every student, regardless of ability, receives individualized curricular and instructional support.

- Students with disabilities participate in educational experiences in the same environments (e.g., general education classroom, school building, community at large) as their classmates who do not have disabilities.

Every adult in the classroom must have a clear understanding of these characteristics of an inclusive classroom to work together and effectively support the learning and growth of all students, especially the most fragile. Often, students model the behavior, attitudes, and actions of adults; adults are the role models for what is and is not acceptable. Teachers must promote a shared understanding of how all students are to treat one another. This is the first step in moving toward inclusive education.

In inclusion-oriented schools and classrooms, the community of faculty and staff is continuously reflecting on practices related to how all members of the environment work together, are valued, and move toward individual and collective goals. Members of inclusion-oriented schools are never complacent; rather, they are in a continuous cycle of reflection and improvement.

Although increasing numbers of students with disabilities receive part or all of their educational experiences in general education settings, this does not necessarily mean that they are being included as members of the community. As many adults know or have experienced themselves, placement alone does not equate with belonging. Broer, Doyle, and Giangreco (2005) interviewed 16 young adults with severe intellectual disabilities about their public school experiences of being "included" while receiving one-to-one support from a paraprofessional for extended periods of time. All of the young people reported feelings of isolation and loneliness. They may have been physically present in general education schools and classrooms, but they were rarely included in classroom life. One said, "I didn't feel like I was part of the group...I feel like I was on the outside" (p. 421). Another stated, "When I was in school I had my own little world; I was in my own little world there" (p. 421). The lack of clarity about the roles of the classroom teachers and the paraprofessionals inadvertently contributed to the students' isolation.

As the number of skilled paraprofessionals in schools increases, their roles and responsibilities continue to evolve and become more specialized and more comprehensive. The changing, complex nature of the paraprofessional's role and the importance of paraprofessionals in the lives of all students in inclusion-oriented classrooms make introductory and ongoing training and supervision of paraprofessionals necessary. The purpose of this book is to support that learning and growth within the context of a team. This means that the teacher and the paraprofessional should work through the activities in this book together, rather than the teacher simply handing the book to the paraprofessional. The format of this book is highly interactive. As the role of the paraprofessional is adjusted through discussions and interactive decision making, so too will the roles of the classroom teacher and special education teacher be clarified. The content of this book is intended to be a source of mutual dialogue, growth, and change.

Reflection

Reflection is the heart of good educational decision making. Throughout this text, team members will be encouraged to take time to engage in individual, professional reflection as a way to understand the principles at a deeply personal level. The reflections will encourage each member of the team to take the perspective of others.

- Who are the students and adults in our school community who are marginalized?

- What must it feel like to them?

- Is that the experience I want for any member(s) of my community?

Note: If you actually name the members of your community identified by these questions, the situation will become more real to you, and your team is much more likely to take action.

A Paraprofessional's Reflection

I have worked as a paraprofessional with students who have disabilities for more than 5 years. I became a paraprofessional because I liked working with middle school students, but I didn't want the full responsibilities of being a teacher. I wanted to be able to go in the classroom, do my job, and then go home without having all of the after-school planning and meetings that teachers have to deal with.

My job has changed a lot over the past few years. Now all of the paraprofessionals in my school receive training on all sorts of things, like role clarification, specific reading and math programs, and behavior management strategies. The training has been really helpful. The district office people are pretty clear that even though we are getting more training, it doesn't mean we're teachers. The training helps us support the teachers, but it is still their job to decide what strategies to use and when. They are supposed to tell us what and how to do things.

I know we have a long way to go. There are still a lot of times when I have to fly by the seat of my pants because the teachers haven't done their planning, but I think things are beginning to improve. During one training session, we were encouraged to ask questions in a way that reminds the teachers that we're waiting for their directions. Now, instead of pretending that I know what to do, I have learned to say, "So, how is Jonathan going to participate in this activity?" or "How can I be helpful during this reading activity?" Though it may seem simple, these two questions have made a world of difference in my daily life at work. The teachers I work with say that they appreciate the reminders.

WHO ARE PARAPROFESSIONALS?

The No Child Left Behind (NCLB) Act of 2001 (PL 107-110) defines a paraprofessional as "an individual who is employed in a preschool, elementary school, or secondary school under the supervision of a certified or licensed teacher, including individuals employed in language instruction educational programs, special education, or migrant education" (§ 119). The reauthorization of the Individuals with Disabilities Education Improvement Act (IDEA) of 2004 (PL 108-446) and the passage of NCLB suggest that the federal government recognizes the need for highly qualified people to be working in public schools. In fact, though IDEA 2004 allows for the use of paraprofessionals and assistants who are "appropriately trained and supervised…to be used to assist in the provision of special education and related services for children with disabilities" (20 U.S.C., § 1412), it also states that the "paraprofessional provides assistive service, [and] does not serve as a substitute for appropriately trained personnel" (281-41.10[1][b][c]I.A.C.). It is clear that the intention of the law is to provide training and supervision to unlicensed personnel to enable them to assist licensed personnel (e.g., classroom teachers, special education teachers, related services personnel) in meeting the educational needs of children and youth.

Interestingly, NCLB tied federal funding to training by using the term *appropriately trained personnel* to apply to paraprofessionals assisting students in need of Title I services, not to those assisting students requiring special education services. For paraprofessionals who are hired with Title I funding, the requirements are fairly clear: These paraprofessionals must 1) have a secondary diploma or its recognized equivalent, 2) hold an associate's degree or higher, and 3) meet rigorous standards of quality and be able to demonstrate that knowledge in assisting with instruction in reading, writing, and mathematics (U.S. Department of Education, 2002, 2007).

It would seem logical to apply the same criteria to students receiving special education services who also require the part- or full-time support of a paraprofessional. Indeed, many school districts around the nation have chosen to apply the NCLB criteria to all paraprofessionals for several reasons: 1) The criteria are logical, 2) they support best educational practices, and 3) they offer increased personnel flexibility. In addition, as many paraprofessionals are employed to support students with the most significant learning challenges, they need to be highly qualified. If a paraprofessional is hired through a combination of local funds, Title I funds, and special education funds, this increases the types of students the paraprofessional can support.

Many people acknowledge that initial training and follow-up planning and supervision of paraprofessionals is deficient or nonexistent in many schools. However, this is not due to a lack of information, research, or training materials. In fact, between 2000 and 2007, more than 100 publications were generated on issues related to the use of paraprofessionals in supporting students with disabilities (*Selected Paraeducator References,* n.d.). I believe that the lack of training is a result of the speed with which things change in schools, increased demands placed on school personnel, and lack of sufficient funding for supportive and comprehensive implementation efforts.

A variety of job titles are used throughout the United States to refer to personnel who function in the role of paraprofessional. These titles include *paraeducator, educational aide, instructional assistant, teacher's assistant, individualized learning assistant, independent living skills assistant,* and others. In this book, I use the term *paraprofessionals* to refer to school employees who work under the supervision of a certified teacher or other professional staff member (e.g., speech-language pathologist, physical therapist) to complete a variety of instructional and noninstructional tasks. What is the term used in your school? Do the paraprofessionals find the term to be respectful and to accurately reflect the work they do?

Paraprofessionals do not work alone in the classroom; they are members of one or more education teams that always include certified educators or related services personnel (e.g., physical therapist, occupational therapist). The March 2004 Title I Nonregulatory Guidance document explicitly stated, "Because paraprofessionals provide instructional support, they should not be introducing to students new skills, concepts, or academic content" (p. 1). Of course, this raises the question of who are "qualified" personnel. According to federal regulations, qualified personnel are those who have met the identified licensing requirements to earn "certification, licensing, registration, or other comparable requirements that apply to the area in which the individuals are providing special education or related services" (*Code of Federal Regulations,* 1999). In addition, an entire body of educational research has developed around the use, overuse, and misuse of paraprofessional personnel. To that end, it is my intention that educational teams led by certified personnel and who are teaching students in inclusion-oriented classrooms use the material in this book. It is not my intention that this material be used in a way that would 1) encourage team members to allow paraprofessionals to work in isolation or 2) replace general and special educators. Therefore, it would be inappropriate to use this book to train paraprofessionals in isolation. Doing so would do more harm than good because paraprofessionals would then be equipped with knowledge and skills that the educators may or may not have. The information in this book necessitates conversations and problem solving, as paraprofessional training affects the whole classroom community. The ongoing instructional leadership and direct involvement of certified teachers is critical to the successful training of paraprofessionals.

WHAT ARE THE PARAPROFESSIONAL'S RESPONSIBILITIES IN AN INCLUSION-ORIENTED CLASSROOM?

Paraprofessionals assist students and teachers in inclusion-oriented classroom communities in a variety of ways. They provide direct and indirect support to the classroom teacher, to individual students, and to all the students in the classroom, and they engage in positive interactions with other members of the instructional team (e.g., educators, therapists, other paraprofessionals). Caring and supportive school personnel, including paraprofessionals, can make the difference in a student's ability or inability to manage stress, avoid self-destructive behavior, and grow into an emotionally healthy adult.

Paraprofessionals' specific responsibilities may include preparing materials or making adaptations to support students' learning, providing assistance with instructional delivery, implementing teacher-designed individualized instruction, and assisting with classroom management. Take a moment to review Para Form 2: The Paraprofessional's Responsibilities, located in the Para Forms appendix. Which responsibilities do you anticipate paraprofessional(s) on your team will perform? Are there some responsibilities that would be more interesting to learn about than others? Are there additional responsibilities that might be included under the paraprofessional's noninstructional or instructional responsibilities? Are there tasks that you initially identified for the paraprofessional, but now realize are actually teacher responsibilities?

In preparation for a conversation among team members, each person should review The Paraprofessional's Responsibilities. Have someone place a checkmark in the column labeled *Training* if the paraprofessional needs training in that area. Review and discuss your thoughts about the paraprofessional's responsibilities with your team members. Remember that the paraprofessional is a valued team member and should be part of the discussion. After the team has reached agreement on the specific tasks that are and are not the paraprofessional's responsibilities, rank those tasks that require immediate training. Develop a training plan that 1) outlines the focus of the training; 2) identifies which certified member of the team will provide the training, monitoring, and feedback; and 3) indicates when the training will occur. This discussion will help every member of your team develop a clear understanding of the paraprofessional's role and responsibilities.

Although paraprofessionals fulfill many essential duties related to instruction, they should not be responsible for the initial design, development, or evaluation of instructional procedures for any students. This is a key difference between the responsibilities of certified personnel and those of paraprofessionals: Certified personnel are always responsible for the design, implementation, and evaluation of instruction. Although paraprofessionals can contribute ideas and suggestions and assist with the implementation of instruction, they should not be held accountable for the quality of instruction design. The Individuals with Disabilities Education Act (IDEA) Amendments of 1997 (PL 105-17) addressed this issue directly by stating that paraprofessionals "are to be used to assist in the provisions of special education and related services" (§ 1412). Certified staff (e.g., general and special educators, speech-language pathologists, occupational therapists, physical therapists) are responsible for the initial design of the instructional plans (i.e., lesson plans). They are also responsible for providing paraprofessionals with the necessary information, training, instructional plans, and supervision to fulfill instructionally related responsibilities. Paraprofessionals are also not responsible for assessment and decision making. Although paraprofessionals may assist in the collection of some types of assessment information, certified staff maintain the responsibility for assessment and decision making at all times. Because the specific roles and responsibilities of paraprofessionals may vary from one school to the next, every instructional team should discuss and clarify the expectations associated with a specific classroom.

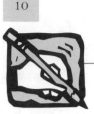

Reflection

- Is the paraprofessional on our team acting as a support to the team, or have we inadvertently relegated too many instructional responsibilities to the paraprofessional?

- What do we need to do to remedy this situation?

WHAT TRAINING AND SUPPORT DO PARAPROFESSIONALS REQUIRE?

The most common form of training paraprofessionals receive is informal and unstructured (Causton-Theoharis & Malgren, 2005; Devlin, 2005; Ghere & York-Barr, 2007; Quilty, 2007). Some teams use an *embedded*, or on-the-job, approach to providing training (Ghere, York-Barr, & Sommerness, 2002). Regardless of the training format used, certain content areas are extremely helpful for paraprofessionals and teachers. These include role clarification, school and classroom orientation, positive behavior support (PBS), specific ways to support classroom teachers and special educators, implementation of specific instruction strategies and accommodations, and how to read and implement teacher-designed lesson plans. In addition, paraprofessionals can be taught how to advocate for themselves in a manner that prompts teachers to realign their expectations based on the responsibilities that align with each person's role. For example, it is the teacher's role to make the decision regarding specific instructional strategies and student grouping arrangements. A paraprofessional might ask, "How should I support Kerri during this activity?" or "What is the grouping arrangement?" The teacher makes instructional decisions while the paraprofessional helps with implementation.

Following are two activities that can be used for role clarification. The activities are intended to be used with a large group of several educational teams, but they can be adapted for use with just one team. Read both of the activity descriptions and choose the one that is best suited to your team.

ACTIVITY 1

Basic Role Differentiation

This activity provides team members with an opportunity to examine their individual roles and responsibilities in a rather general way. It should be carried out in a playful atmosphere in which creativity is encouraged. Many teams find this activity to be a nonthreatening way to begin exploring the issues related to paraprofessional training. Table 1.1 depicts and describes some symbols that may prove helpful during this activity. These symbols are commonly used by teams to depict important attributes for paraprofessionals, general educators, and special educators.

Table 1.1. Commonly used symbols for Activity 1

Symbol	Paraprofessional	General educator	Special educator
Big heart	Cares for members of the community, including students and their families, faculty, and staff	Cares for members of the community, including students and their families, faculty, and staff	Cares for members of the community, including students and their families, faculty, and staff
Ready smile	Has a kind smile for all	Has a kind smile for all	Has a kind smile for all
Feet with wheels or running shoes	Is always on the move to implement teacher-designed plans	Is always running to keep up with the latest issues of curriculum and instruction Moves fast to keep all students interested	Is always running to keep up with various members of the team Is well organized
Big ears	Listens well to instruction and feedback from teachers	Listens actively to the needs of many adults and students	Listens to the needs of team members and integrates the information into daily plans
Checkmark	Corrects papers well	Designs assignments Interprets assessment information	Designs individualized assessments Administers and evaluates formal and informal assessments to inform student programming
Juggling balls	Implements teacher-designed instruction	Designs, implements, and evaluates instruction for all students Designs, implements, and evaluates curricular adaptations for all students	Designs, implements, and evaluates instruction for students with disabilities Designs, implements, and evaluates curricular adaptations for students with disabilities Designs and develops student-specific accommodations
Flip-top head	Is open-minded to suggestions and new ideas from other team members	Is open-minded to suggestions and new ideas from other team members Able to consider multiple perspectives	Is open-minded to suggestions and new ideas from other team members Able to consider multiple perspectives in student planning

1a. Create-a-Paraprofessional

As a team, brainstorm the qualities that each member associates with an ideal paraprofessional. Identify all of the characteristics, skills, and abilities that everyone associates with this ideal paraprofessional. Use the attributes to draw the ideal paraprofessional. For a filled-in example, see Figure 1.1, Create-a-Paraprofessional worksheet (for a blank version of this worksheet, see Activity 1a: Create-a-Paraprofessional, found in the Activities appendix).

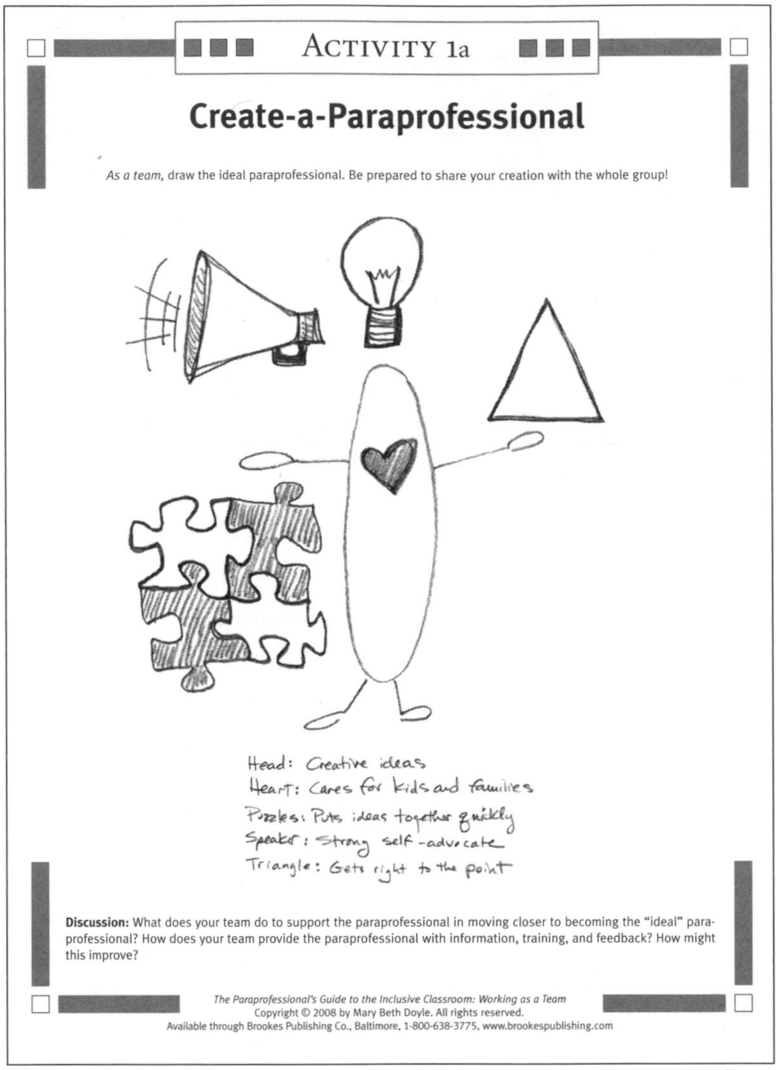
ACTIVITY 1a

Create-a-Paraprofessional

As a team, draw the ideal paraprofessional. Be prepared to share your creation with the whole group!

Head: Creative ideas
Heart: Cares for kids and families
Puzzles: Puts ideas together quickly
Speaker: Strong self-advocate
Triangle: Gets right to the point

Discussion: What does your team do to support the paraprofessional in moving closer to becoming the "ideal" paraprofessional? How does your team provide the paraprofessional with information, training, and feedback? How might this improve?

Figure 1.1. Example of Activity 1a: Create-a-Paraprofessional.

1b. Create-a-General Educator

As a team, brainstorm qualities that each member associates with an ideal general educator. Identify all of the characteristics, skills, and abilities that everyone associates with this ideal general educator. Use the attributes to draw the ideal general education teacher. For a filled-in example, see Figure 1.2, Create-a-General Educator worksheet (for a blank version of this worksheet, see Activity 1b: Create-a-General Educator, found in the Activities appendix).

1c. Create-a-Special Educator

As a team, brainstorm qualities that each member associates with an ideal special educator. Identify the characteristics, skills, and abilities that everyone associates with this ideal special educator. Use the attributes to draw the ideal special educator. For a filled-in example, see Figure 1.3, Create-a-Special Educator worksheet (for a blank version of this worksheet, see Activity 1c: Create-a-Special Educator, found in the Activities appendix).

ACTIVITY 2

Activity Debriefing

After each team member has had the opportunity to draw his or her ideal team members, display the creations and ask a member from each team to describe his or her creation. Then debrief the activity as a whole group; use Activity 2: Activity Debriefing locat-

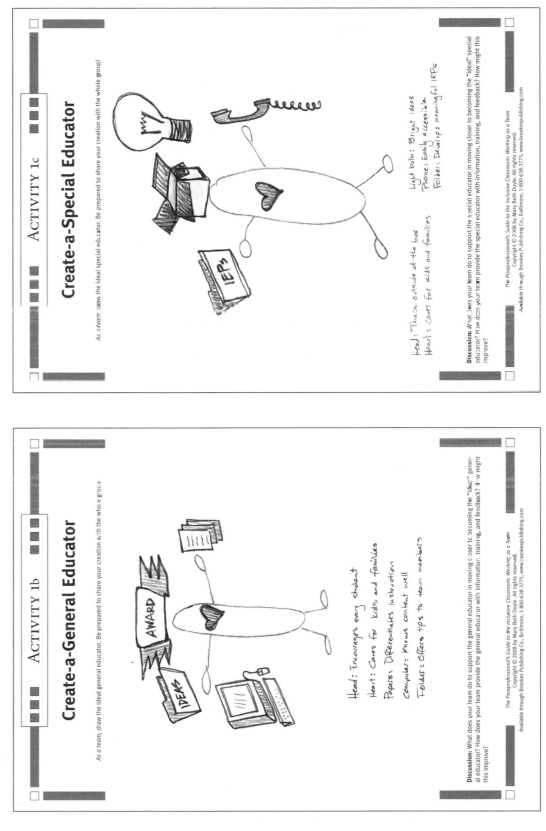

ACTIVITY 1c

Create-a-Special Educator

As a team, draw the ideal special educator. Be prepared to share your creation with the whole group!

Head: Think outside of the box
Heart: Cares for kids and families

Light bulb: Bright ideas
Phone: Easily accessible
Folder: Develops meaningful IEPs

IEPs

Discussion: What does your team do to support the special educator in moving closer to becoming the "ideal" special educator? How does your team provide the special educator with information, training, and feedback? How might this improve?

The Paraprofessional's Guide to the Inclusive Classroom: Working as a Team
Copyright © 2008 by Mary Beth Doyle. All rights reserved.
Available through Brookes Publishing Co., Baltimore, 1-800-638-3775, www.brookespublishing.com

Figure 1.3. Example of Activity 1c: Create-a-Special Educator.

ACTIVITY 1b

Create-a-General Educator

As a team, draw the ideal general educator. Be prepared to share your creation with the whole group.

AWARD

IDEAS

Head: Encourages every student
Heart: Cares for kids and families
Papers: Differentiates instruction
Computer: Knows content well
Folder: Offers tips to team members

Discussion: What does your team do to support the general educator in moving closer to becoming the "ideal" general educator? How does your team provide the general educator with information, training, and feedback? How might this improve?

The Paraprofessional's Guide to the Inclusive Classroom: Working as a Team
Copyright © 2008 by Mary Beth Doyle. All rights reserved.
Available through Brookes Publishing Co., Baltimore, 1-800-638-3775, www.brookespublishing.com

Figure 1.2. Example of Activity 1b: Create-a-General Educator.

ed in the Activities appendix to record some of the group's observations. As team members describe their creations, patterns will emerge that reflect the skills, abilities, and characteristics that are necessary for every person, regardless of his or her role in the classroom, to display when working with children and youth. Typically, these characteristics are fairly general. They might include being good at listening, skilled at planning, responsible, or able to juggle multiple responsibilities at the same time. The next pattern that usually emerges reflects skills and abilities that are specific to each person's role. For example, characteristics of an excellent special educator include the ability to individualize instruction using very specific instructional techniques. A skilled general educator can differentiate instruction for a wide variety of students. An excellent paraprofessional can implement instruction under the supervision of the special educator.

In some circumstances, a team may not identify significant role differences. If this is the case, the facilitator should make a mental note. If team members cannot identify the specific knowledge, skills, and abilities that each member contributes, they are less likely to be able to leverage those contributions when necessary throughout the school year. They are also more likely to assign the paraprofessional the work of licensed personnel because they fail to see and acknowledge the differences in roles. In such cases, it is critical for the team to target role clarification as an area for professional development.

Conclude this activity with a discussion of the similarities and differences in roles. Acknowledge that a strong collaborative team is one that brings together personnel who have a shared agenda and complementary skills.

ACTIVITY 3

Role Clarification with a Twist

This activity is meant to help team members who have more experience with collaboration to focus on role clarification more quickly. The activity initially focuses on general clarification and quickly moves into the identification of the necessary tools for supporting team members in meeting their responsibilities.

Materials (per group):

- One large brown paper bag
- One bag of craft materials (e.g., colored paper, cloth material, buttons, glitter)
- One pair of scissors
- One glue stick or roll of tape
- One set of markers

Steps:

1. Divide participants into role-alike groups (i.e., a group of general educators, a group of special educators, and a group of paraprofessionals) of five people each.

2. Distribute one set of materials to each group.

3. Direct the general educators to use their materials (e.g., markers, glue, glitter, buttons) to create an image of the ideal paraprofessional on the outside of the bag. Direct the special educators to use their materials to create an image of the ideal general educator on the outside of the bag. Direct the paraprofessionals to do the same regarding the ideal special educator on the outside of the bag. (*Note: Any combination of team and subject will work, as long as team members are creating an image of someone other than themselves. For example, a team of paraprofessionals could create an image of the ideal general educator or special educator.*)

4. Encourage participants to have fun with this activity by using creative symbols to depict important characteristics. For example, they might draw roller skates on the feet if quick movement is important or glue on large ears if listening is important.

5. When teams have finished, invite each team to share its creation.

Conclude this portion of the activity by asking team members to compare and contrast the similarities and differences among the images of ideal team members created on the bags.

It is likely that teams will enjoy the first part of this activity. Now it is time to add a more serious component. Ask teams to give their bag to the appropriate role group so that the paraprofessionals receive the ideal paraprofessional creation and the general and special educators receive the creations based on their roles. Instruct each team to list all of the knowledge, skills, abilities, and dispositions they need in order to accomplish their daily responsibilities. Discuss these lists with the whole group. (You can use Activity 3: Role Clarification with a Twist, located in the Activities appendix, as a master transparency.) Ask the group to note the knowledge, skills, and abilities that are similar and different.

APPLICATION AND REVIEW OF THE LAW

After engaging in one of the previous activities, teams should have a clear understanding of the roles and responsibilities of licensed personnel and of paraprofessionals. Using Table 1.2, Applying the Law, have teams identify the areas in which they need a clearer understanding of differential roles. Have them indicate how they will address these needs as a team.

Paraprofessional Self-Advocacy

As both the text and the preceding activities make clear, the roles of paraprofessionals are distinctly different from those of classroom teachers and special education teachers. In many actual school situations, both teachers and paraprofessionals can quickly distinguish between their different responsibilities. Yet, it is not at all uncommon for paraprofessionals to assume the initial teaching responsibilities of licensed personnel when supporting students with the most complex learning challenges. It is important to note that this occurs not out of any ill intention on the part of teachers but because classrooms are complex and demanding environments. General education teachers juggle many responsibilities, so when nonoptimal pedagogical decisions for a student with disabilities are made, it is very often unintentional.

As paraprofessionals, you can and should take action to correct this situation as a form of self-advocacy. *Self-advocacy* is the ability to communicate your needs to another person in a kind, respectful manner. If a licensed teacher has inadvertently asked you to do tasks that are not appropriate to your role, ask clarifying questions that will remind the teacher of your appropriate role. For example, when you are asked to facilitate an individual or a small-group lesson, you should expect that the teacher has already developed an instructional plan and that the instructional strategies are ones that you have already been taught. For further clarification, you might ask such questions as the following:

- What is the instructional outcome of this lesson?

- How should I address the outcome? What specific strategies should I use?

- What evidence will the students produce that they have achieved the outcome?

If you are unclear about the strategy you should use, ask, "Will you model that strategy for me before I use it with the students?" Modeling is a good example of embedded training.

Table 1.2. Applying the law

Laws regarding paraprofessionals	Inappropriate practices on our team	Desired practices
Paraprofessionals assist in the provision of special education services.	*Paraprofessional takes the lead with instruction in classes with students with disabilities.*	*Teachers provide instructional leadership.* *Teachers provide training to paraprofessionals.* *Teachers monitor and give feedback to paraprofessionals.*
Paraprofessionals receive appropriate training.	*Paraprofessional receives general school district training on policies and practices about days off and confidentiality.*	*Paraprofessional receives specific training in instructional approaches to use with individual students.*
Paraprofessionals are supervised by appropriate personnel.	*Paraprofessional receives no formal supervision.*	*Supervision is tied to training.* *Supervision occurs after the teacher has modeled a specific approach.* *Supervision occurs under actual circumstances.*

Because your team is using this book to improve your collective work, I encourage paraprofessionals to use Para Form 3: Advocacy Skills for Paraprofessionals: Asking for What You Need, located in the Para Forms appendix. You should assume a leadership role in specifying some of the training.

Throughout the remainder of this book, there will be structured opportunities for you to assume the role of self-advocate by continually reminding the licensed personnel of your roles and responsibilities. Offering gentle, carefully worded reminders can assist the team in shifting from old patterns of behavior and support all parties in meeting their individual responsibilities.

 # Reflection

Teachers: Would it be acceptable for a classroom teacher or a special education teacher to assume the responsibilities of a district administrator but be paid the salary of a classroom teacher? How might it feel to be in the shoes of a paraprofessional who is assuming teaching responsibilities?

Paraprofessionals: How might it feel to be a teacher who has historically had her own eighth-grade classroom but now also has several students with disabilities and a paraprofessional to assist? What adjustments might the teacher need to make?

CONCLUSION

The focus of this chapter has been on the clarification of roles and responsibilities of paraprofessionals, classroom teachers, special educators, and other team members. Such clarification increases the likelihood that educational programs for students will be well designed and appropriately supported. It also allows team members to act in a coordinated and focused manner, ensuring that nothing is overlooked. Role clarification is the basis for building classroom communities in which adults work together to meet the needs of all students.

2

The Inclusive Classroom
Being a Member of the Team

Objectives

- Get to know individual team members
- Develop the paraprofessional's daily schedule
- Adjust to the changing needs of an inclusive classroom
- Identify specific daily responsibilities affecting the classroom
- Examine the effects of paraprofessional proximity
- Use self-advocacy skills to clarify responsibilities

Five of the most common questions asked by education team members consist of the following:

1. What is a team?

2. Who am I working with?

3. Who is responsible for what?

4. What is my daily schedule?

5. How do I ask for what I need?

Using the knowledge presented in this chapter, the members of your team will have the opportunity to become better acquainted with one another and work as a team to develop an initial schedule for the paraprofessional. Team members will learn to request the specific support they need to fulfill their responsibilities on the team.

ACTIVITY 4

What Is a Team?

Think about teams you have been a member of (e.g., sports teams, social clubs) that have yielded positive experiences for you. What characteristics of those teams made the experiences positive? What did you do, and how did you feel, as a member of a team? It is likely that the team had a shared vision, meaning, and purpose. Each member of the team came together with the intention of pursuing the same goals. Members of sports teams join together to participate in the sport; social clubs get together to chat with each other. Membership and participation were probably reinforcing on some level for each person. In addition, each member had something to contribute to the collective goal.

Now think about a group activity in which you have participated (e.g., attending a lecture, mall walking). What characteristics of that arrangement of people made it a group? How did you feel as a member of the group? It is likely that each member had responsibilities, but it is also likely that each had a different motivation for being in that group (e.g., some mall walkers may have been interested in losing weight, others in spending time with friends). The closeness among group members was probably much less intense than closeness among members of a team. It is, of course, important to people's well-being to have access to both arrangements—teams and groups. When referring to an educational team, however, it is important to differentiate between the two.

Teams are intentional groups of people who come together for a common purpose. Giangreco (1996) defined a team as "two or more people who share a common set of values, beliefs, and assumptions about education, children, families, and professionals" (p. 4). Can you describe the values, beliefs, and assumptions that your team has agreed to regarding education, children, families, and professionals? If your team has not defined these values, assumptions, and beliefs, it is likely that it is functioning more as a group. To become a team, members must take the time to clarify collective values, beliefs, and assumptions about education, children, families, and professionals. Write these beliefs on a piece of chart paper and hang it in a place that will be highly visible during team meetings. Link the value statements with actions. Here are some examples:

- We believe that our classroom should be a safe and welcoming space; therefore, we will not raise our voices in anger.

- We believe that all students can learn; therefore, we will adapt the curriculum and instruction to support individual students.

- We believe that every member of the educational team has important contributions to make; therefore, we will demonstrate respect by aligning our expectations with each person's responsibilities.

Successfully completing this step increases the likelihood that adults and students will feel welcomed and supported. Throughout the year when decisions need to be made, formally review your team's shared set of values, beliefs, and assumptions and ask the team, "How does this issue and our response to it align with our shared values, beliefs, and assumptions?" Keep in mind that even the best of teams face challenges that press the members to examine and reexamine their shared values, beliefs, and assumptions. These examinations can be very helpful in strengthening the team. Team members need to engage in any challenging conversations with each other in a respectful manner, focusing on the issue at hand as it relates to their shared understandings of education, children, families, and professionals.

WHO AM I WORKING WITH?

At this point, each member of your team probably knows at least the names of the other school personnel and is familiar with some of the students with whom he or she will be working on a daily basis. Throughout the school year, your team (i.e., the general educator, special educator, and paraprofessional) will share the responsibility of facilitating the learning and growth of every student in the classroom. Because students in inclusive classrooms have such a wide variety of needs and abilities, your team must work together, sharing ideas and learning to support the students as well as one another.

Having a semistructured way to get to know one another or to welcome a new team member might help everyone feel more comfortable. In fact, Riggs (2004) found that paraprofessionals want teachers and other team members to get to know them on a personal level. They want teachers to know their names, interests, backgrounds, and experiences. Para Form 4: Welcome Interview worksheet, located in the Para Forms appendix, can be used to assist the members of your team in getting to know one another. By completing this interview as a team, members can learn more about one another and can develop an initial understanding of the paraprofessional's specific roles and responsibilities. Because paraprofessionals frequently interact with extended team members (e.g., speech-language pathologist, occupational therapist, physical therapist), these team members might also participate in this interview process. Their participation increases the likelihood that every member of the team will have a clear understanding of the roles and responsibilities of the paraprofessional in particular. Arrange a time when everyone on the team can meet and enjoy conversation with the new team members. Early investment in relationships will yield long-term benefits.

A Special Education Teacher's Reflection

This was my tenth year as a special educator at the high school level. I was responsible for five paraprofessionals and 15 students with disabilities. If I have learned anything over the years, it is that organization is a must! Before everyone comes back in September, I organize information in two ways. First, I make a master list of my students and their goals and accommodations. Using that information, I make individual packets of materials to give to the teachers and paraprofessionals during the in-service days just before school begins. Each packet includes an instructional chart listing the student's name, goals, literacy information, and accommodations for each class. I also include any other important information, such as PBS plans or allergies.

Second, I meet with all of the paraprofessionals during the first week of school. I try to set the tone for the year and clarify roles and responsibilities. It may seem like a lot of work to prepare this way, but it isn't any different from planning units or lessons for a classroom of students. Now the paraprofessionals have come to expect all of this information from me, and as a result our team is really solid. I never would have guessed that my level of preparation would have such a positive impact on my relationship with the paraprofessionals.

Another thing that is really important to our team is communication, both written and verbal. I follow up all of the written information with regularly scheduled meetings. We meet for about 30 minutes every other week for training in specific teaching techniques. I spend 20 minutes teaching all of the paraprofessionals a new skill and 10 minutes on scheduling. The scheduling allows us to determine a time when I can observe the paraprofessionals implementing a teaching technique or management skill that I've taught them during the session or a previous one.

My next goal is to meet with the general education teachers to think about different ways we can use paraprofessional support. For example, instead of assigning paraprofessionals to individual students, I think we would be more successful if we assigned them to classroom teachers.

WHO IS RESPONSIBLE FOR WHAT?

Let me clearly state that classroom teachers and special educators are responsible to design, implement, and evaluate all instruction. Paraprofessionals can assist with aspects of instruction that have already been planned. They can support and tutor individual and small groups of students. Paraprofessionals can also prepare materials, complete clerical tasks, and manage a variety of classroom-related tasks to free up the general and special education teachers to do more direct instruction.

The quickest way to determine whether or not what the paraprofessional is doing is appropriate within the confines of his or her role is to use the "Would it be okay?" test. This simple test can be administered by any member of the team in just about any situation in which it is perplexing to define responsibilities. Simply answer the question "If the student whom the paraprofessional is supporting did not have a disability, would it be okay for the paraprofessional to be providing the same type of support on an ongoing basis?" Using this "test" increases the likelihood that team members are maintaining their responsibilities. When approaching situations in this manner, it is also important to maintain the underlying assumption that any apparent mismatch between stated and actual roles and responsibilities is probably not intentional; it is more likely simply a mistake of some sort. This mismatch happens often when paraprofessionals are given too much responsibility for the educational programs for individual students. When the paraprofessional recognizes the mistake, he or she should approach the appropriate person and say, "I'm not comfortable with my responsibilities in this situation." In the majority of situations, the team member will be thankful for the acknowledgment and respond appropriately. Information on paraprofessional responsibilities related to specific topics (e.g., PBS, curriculum, instruction) will be presented throughout the remainder of the text.

WHAT IS MY DAILY SCHEDULE?

To prepare a daily schedule for the paraprofessional, the classroom teacher should list the following:

1. Daily classroom schedule

2. Daily tasks that need to be completed

3. Areas in which the teacher needs assistance

4. Areas in which the teacher would like assistance

5. Areas in which the teacher does not want assistance

Using Para Form 5: Classroom Routine worksheet, the classroom teacher fills out the typical daily activity schedule in the first two columns (time and activity). (See Figure 2.1 for a filled-in version of an elementary example and Figure 2.2 for a filled-in version of a high school example in this chapter; a blank version of this worksheet appears in the Para Forms appendix.) In the third column (tasks), the teacher writes in the tasks that are generally associated with each activity. In the fourth and fifth columns, the teacher checks the items for which he or she wants or needs the assistance of a paraprofessional. When the teacher does this, the initial responsibilities of the paraprofessional begin to emerge. This set of decisions can actually be difficult for a classroom teacher who is accustomed to doing

■■■ PARA FORM 5 ■■■

Classroom Routine

Directions: In the first and second column, enter the time and activity. In the third column, enter the typical tasks associated with each activity. In the fourth and fifth columns, check who will complete the tasks: the teacher, the paraprofessional, or both. As a team, discuss this routine.

Time	Activity	Tasks	Teacher	Paraprofessional	Comments
7:30	Arrive	Check mailbox Check e-mail Arrange math center Pull out homework basket Arrange morning choice games	✓ ✓	✓ ✓ ✓ ✓	Given a prepared list, the paraprofessional arranges math center activities.
7:50	Students arrive	Hang up coats Welcome each child Hand in paper and notes Free choice time	✓ ✓ ✓	✓ ✓ ✓	
8:10	Meeting	Calendar Math problems Dictation correction Current events	✓ ✓ ✓ ✓		The paraprofessional arranges the activities for the reading group.
8:30	Reading groups	Group and individual reading	✓	✓	One group at a time, each implements teacher-directed instruction
9:45	Student snack			✓	Supervised by the paraprofessional
10:10	Math	Single- and double-digit addition	✓	✓	The teacher gives initial instruction and follow up with groups of three. The paraprofessional supervises students at the math center.
11:10	Lunch	Gather lunches and coats for outside recess			

Figure 2.1. Elementary school example of Para Form 5: Classroom Routine.

all of the daily tasks associated with teaching by him- or herself, so the special educator might need to provide some assistance to the classroom teacher. For example, the special education teacher might suggest that the paraprofessional supervise the students while they are arriving in the classroom so the teacher can make parent contacts or review the lesson plans. Or, the classroom teacher might decide to have the paraprofessional join in greeting and welcoming each student into the classroom every day. Making deliberate decisions such as these and talking about them with the paraprofessional is very helpful. This seemingly simple decision is particularly important in situations in which a paraprofessional has been assigned to a classroom because of the specific needs of an individual student with disabilities, because it clearly communicates the teacher's expectations to the paraprofessional and eliminates any guessing or assumptions on the part of the paraprofessional.

ACTIVITIES 5 AND 6

Developing and Discussing the Paraprofessional's Daily Schedule

Using Para Form 5: Classroom Routine worksheet (located in the Para Forms appendix), the teacher should develop a daily schedule for the classroom, highlighting activities for which assistance is absolutely necessary and activities for which assistance would be helpful but is not critical. Next, the teacher should finalize a daily schedule for the paraprofessional that includes specific roles and responsibilities using Activity 5: The

■■■ PARA FORM 5 ■■■

Classroom Routine

Directions: In the first and second column, enter the time and activity. In the third column, enter the typical tasks associated with each activity. In the fourth and fifth columns, check who will complete the tasks: the teacher, the paraprofessional, or both. As a team, discuss this routine.

Time	Activity	Tasks	Teacher	Paraprofessional	Comments
8:30	Students arrive Attendance Agenda written on the board as students take out their materials	Agenda written on the board as students take out their materials	✓		The paraprofessional enters + or – in grade book indicating whether or not it was handed in.
		Attendance	✓	✓	
		Collect homework	✓	✓	
8:35	Introduction of content	Direct instruction	✓		The paraprofessional monitors all students and redirects when necessary
9:10	Practice	Group or individual work related to application of new ideas	✓	✓	Monitor and support all students
9:35	Review for homework		✓	✓	Support target student in preparing for transition (e.g. writing down home-work, reviewing schedule for the next class)

Figure 2.2. High school example of Para Form 5: Classroom Routine.

Paraprofessional's Daily Schedule (see Figure 2.3 for a filled-in version of this activity form in this chapter; a blank version of this activity appears in the Activities appendix). This worksheet documents the paraprofessional's schedule and further clarifies the paraprofessional's responsibilities in supporting students with disabilities in the general education classroom. If the paraprofessional's schedule varies from day to day, simply make several copies of the blank schedule and complete one for each day of the week. After the paraprofessional's initial schedule has been developed, discuss the questions presented in the Activity 6: Discussion About the Paraprofessional's Daily Schedule worksheet (see Figure 2.4 for a filled-version in this chapter; a blank version of this activity appears in the Activities appendix). The information generated during this discussion may require a revision of the paraprofessional's initial schedule. After the schedule has been completed, be certain to make a photocopy for each member of your team.

Keep in mind that the paraprofessional's schedule will change as the needs of the students and teachers change. When this happens, the paraprofessional, the special educator, and the general educator should meet to rework the paraprofessional's schedule to reflect the changing needs of the classroom community.

UP-FRONT ISSUES TO REACH CONSENSUS ON

Thus far, the activities in this book have focused on clarifying team expectations about roles and responsibilities, especially those of the paraprofessional. In many situations, either by default or through lack of clarity, the paraprofessional assumes primary responsibility for making instructional decisions for students with disabilities (French, 2001; Giangreco, Broer, & Edelman, 2001; Riggs & Mueller, 2001; Werts, Harris, Tillery, & Roark, 2004). To

ACTIVITY 5

The Paraprofessional's Daily Schedule

Directions: The general educator, the special educator, and the paraprofessional need to work together to develop the paraprofessional's daily schedule. This schedule should reflect the paraprofessional's duties that are related to supporting the general learning environment as well as individual students. After the schedule has been drafted, use Activity 6: Discussion About the Paraprofessional's Daily Schedule to determine whether the schedule needs revision.

Time	Typical class or activity	Paraprofessional's typical responsibilities
8:00	Arrival	Help students with coats and books
	• Lockers, homeroom	Prepare materials for whole class (no direct responsibilities with
	• Hang out with friends	students)
	• Morning activities and class job	
8:45	Reading	Implement small-group lesson developed by classroom teacher
	• Small group	
10:15	Science	Assist student with disabilities participate with peers in the lab
		Monitor all students
11:00	Snacks	Develop materials adaptation, set up learning centers
11:15	Gym	Assist as directed by gym teacher
12:00	Lunch	Scan lunchroom to be certain that student with disabilities is eating
		with peers
1:00	Math	Implement small-group lesson developed by classroom teacher
1:45	Spelling	Review words and dictation with whole class
2:15	Computer class	Assist student with disabilities to activate switch
3:00	School's out!	Help with students' coats and books

The Paraprofessional's Guide to the Inclusive Classroom: Working as a Team

Figure 2.3. Example of Activity 5: The Paraprofessional's Daily Schedule.

avoid this practice, the team should pay particular attention to the responsibilities of each member and address the responsibilities and expectations regarding several important interrelated issues as early as possible in the year: lesson planning, delivery of instruction, proactive and reactive responses to students' behaviors, strategies to promote ongoing communication, and methods of student evaluation. These issues are highlighted in Para Form 6: Up-Front Issues to Reach Consensus On worksheet, located in the Para Forms appendix. When you have completed this worksheet, take a few moments to review your decisions and put them to the "Would it be okay?" test that was described in the previous section. More specific descriptions of these issues are highlighted in the following sections.

Planning

The first two questions on Para Form 6: Up-Front Issues to Reach Consensus On address issues of what role the paraprofessional will play with regard to instructional planning. It is important to note that the options that are given are only those related to the paraprofessional providing assistance to the licensed teacher. This aligns directly with the differences in roles as discussed in the previous section.

Lesson Planning

It is always the responsibility of certified professionals to plan the curriculum and instruction for all students. Typically, general education teachers prepare instruction on a weekly basis and/or on the basis of thematic units. In inclusive classrooms, this does not change. The classroom teacher should maintain the responsibility for designing instruction for all students. When classroom teachers need specific suggestions, advice, or support for designing specialized instructional support to enable a student with disabilities to participate in and benefit from general education, the special educator is responsible for providing that

ACTIVITY 6

Discussion About the Paraprofessional's Daily Schedule

Directions: After the paraprofessionals' daily schedule has been developed, the classroom teacher, the special educator, and the paraprofessional should meet to discuss the question listed on this worksheet. The answer to the question may necessitate an immediate revision of the paraprofessional's daily schedule or a revision in the future.

In reviewing the paraprofessional's daily schedule, to what extent is he or she engaged in activities related only to the student with disabilities?

None of the time		Some of the time		All of the time	
0	1	②	3	④	5

As a team, discuss whether the level of interaction that the paraprofessional has with the student who has a disability is appropriate. Keep in mind that when adults (e.g., paraprofessional, general educator, special educator) remain in close proximity to a student with disabilities, classmates are less likely to approach and interact with the student. As a team, you may discover that is necessary to develop a formal plan to support the student with disabilities in becoming less dependent on the paraprofessional or other adult team members.

Initially, our team had the paraprofessional maintaining all of the responsibilities related to the student with disabilities. This potentially caused problems because the student with the disabilities needs instruction from certified teachers as well as time with peers. After the discussion, we planned a better schedule and will monitor our time.

Figure 2.4. Example of Activity 6: Discussion About the Paraprofessional's Daily Schedule.

direct assistance. Together, the two teachers should design the content and instructional approaches that will enable the student to progress toward his or her individualized educational goals. Then, they plan for how and when support is needed from the paraprofessional. Figure 2.5 shows an example of one way in which a classroom teacher might design a unit of instruction with accommodations for a student with disabilities.

Throughout the school year, it is common and appropriate for the classroom teacher to ask the paraprofessional for suggestions and ideas about content, process, or evaluation strategies that would help the student with disabilities participate in the classroom. In such cases, the paraprofessional should provide whatever suggestions seem appropriate. Both the general education teacher and the paraprofessional must keep in mind that the paraprofessional is providing those suggestions on the basis of her or his experiences with the student, not on the basis of specialized knowledge. This is an important distinction because the ultimate responsibility for decision making belongs to the certified professional. The classroom teacher needs to make the final decision regarding the appropriateness of any instructional accommodation.

Delivery of Instruction

It may be helpful for the paraprofessional to understand the typical flow of instruction so that he or she can be attuned to this flow during lessons. Most teachers use a format based on the following generic cycle:

1. *Purpose:* Teacher states the purpose of the lesson, referring to agenda written on the board

2. *Hook:* Teacher grabs students' attention with something interesting or unusual

Unit title: Solar System	Student: Rick
Objectives: Identify planets in correct order. Describe three characteristics of each planet. Use PowerPoint presentation software to present the information.	IEP Objectives: Identify one planet (Earth). Describe two characteristics of Earth (ie, it is composed of water and land). Follow two-step directions. Act as the timekeeper in a cooperative group.
Grouping arrangements: ✓ Independent ___ Pairs ✓ Small heterogeneous groups ___ Small homogenous groups ✓ Large heterogeneous groups ___ Large homogenous groups	Grouping arrangements: ___ Independent ✓ Pairs ✓ Small heterogeneous groups ___ Small homogenous groups ✓ Large heterogeneous groups ___ Large homogenous groups
✓ Lecture ✓ Reading ✓ Writing ✓ Discussions ✓ Projects ___ Problem solving ___ Other	✓ Lecture ✓ Reading (multilevel instruction) ✓ Writing (multilevel instruction) ✓ Discussions ✓ Projects ___ Problem solving ___ Other
Major unit projects: Poster: Label all planets and place them in their correct order.	Major unit projects: Poster: Use match-to-sample strategy so Rick enters the names of the planets on the computer and prints them off to label his poster. PowerPoint presentation: Work with peer
Materials: Printed PowerPoint slides	Adapted materials: Match-to-sample cards of the planets

Figure 2.5. Example of a unit plan that includes a student's individualized education program (IEP) information.

3. *Review:* Teacher goes over previous concepts to establish a link with new content

4. *Vocabulary:* Teacher introduces new vocabulary terms

5. *Direct instruction:* Teacher provides focused instruction, guidance, or activities to help students master content

6. *Guided practice:* Teacher and paraprofessional move among students to observe, encourage, and offer corrective feedback as students practice and integrate what they have just learned

7. *Independent practice:* Students practice the new concepts, skills, or knowledge without the intervention of others

8. *Assessment:* Teacher carries out assessment for purposes of reteaching where necessary

Within this fairly common teaching cycle, teachers can direct the support work of the paraprofessional by saying, "I'd like you to prepare the adapted vocabulary lists for Amad and Sarah to be used during the review portion of the lesson. Find pictures for the five words I've listed on the sticky note in my plan book and then make flashcards. Finally, help Amad enter them onto the online flashcard program," or "During independent practice time, I will support and redirect all of the students while you set up for the next chemistry lab. The list of items is on my desk," or "During the guided practice phase of this lesson, I'd like you to circulate among the students, paying particular attention to Sam and Tasha. If either of them needs help, please write down what is confusing them, give them the help they need, and leave a note on my desk so I can take it into account during my planning."

The key here is that the teacher is establishing a common professional vocabulary that enhances purposeful communication. The teacher is being deliberate with regard to instruction and thoughtful as to the type of supplemental support that is helpful for individual students and for the classroom as a whole. The teacher is not assuming that the paraprofessional will just *know* what to do. As the teacher and paraprofessional develop a relationship, there will be a predictable flow to both the routine and the instructional flow within each lesson.

It is critical to remember to balance the paraprofessional's responsibilities with the implementation of instruction. Direct services providers are responsible for planning, implementing, and evaluating the educational and related services of each student with an individualized education program (IEP). Paraprofessionals can assist with these responsibilities under the supervision of certified personnel, but they cannot replace the certified personnel. Direct services providers maintain the responsibility for providing paraprofessionals with the appropriate support, training, and feedback so the paraprofessionals can help with the implementation of teacher-designed instruction. Is this happening on your team? The best way to answer this question is to have the courage to ask the paraprofessional, "How do you know what to do with the student(s) you support?" or "How and when do licensed personnel on the team direct your work?"

Questions 3–6 on Para Form 6: Up-Front Issues to Reach Consensus On target the key instructional issues. Note that all of the questions emphasize the role of the paraprofessional as a team member who *assists* with the implementation of instruction. Paraprofessionals are not responsible for all of the implementation of the instruction, nor are they responsible for the design and evaluation of the instruction.

Reflection

How does the paraprofessional on our team know what to do, when to do it, and how to do it?

Proactive and Reactive Responses to Students' Behavior

Most teachers have a code of conduct or a list of classroom expectations that guides students' behavior. This generally includes expectations about how members of the classroom should treat one another, how materials in the room should be used and cared for, and how daily management responsibilities are to be carried out (e.g., attendance, returning homework). The purpose of the expectations is to teach students to respect themselves and other members of their classroom community. Such experiences contribute to the emotional health of the community. When working as a team, it is helpful for the teacher to be explicit about the paraprofessional's role in supporting those classroom expectations. Questions 7–10 on Para Form 6: Up-Front Issues to Reach Consensus On address this issue directly.

Strategies to Promote Ongoing Communication

Communication between the classroom teacher and the paraprofessional is vital. Simple conversations and gestures of welcome can make the difference between a successful professional relationship and isolation of the paraprofessional. The general or special educator might initiate a conversation about a new teaching strategy or resource, share a new idea, or simply welcome the paraprofessional back to school after a break. These types of communication can foster a positive relationship. In addition, team members need to discuss the more formal aspects of communication as related to daily activities with students and interactions with students' families. Questions 11 and 12 on Para Form 6: Up-Front Issues to Reach Consensus On highlight issues related to typical classroom needs and communication with families of students with and without disabilities. It is important for the classroom teacher and the paraprofessional to be clear on how and in what form such communication will take place. In some situations, for example, the classroom teacher maintains all communication with all students' parents, including the parents of students with disabilities. In other situations, the paraprofessional is encouraged to answer parents' questions and maintain formal types of communication. In all cases, the paraprofessional must have a clear understanding of his or her role and of the confidentiality rules surrounding such communication. This is another situation in which it could be helpful to apply the "Would it be okay?" rule: "Would it be okay for nonlicensed personnel to maintain primary communication with the parents of students without disabilities? If not, why not? Why would that be different for students with disabilities?"

Methods of Student Evaluation

Assessment is the process of gathering information about what students know and are able to do in a specific area of focus. The key question when designing an assessment is how to find out what students are learning. There are a variety of ways to do this, including 1) traditional question-and-answer tests in which a teacher determines the number correct; 2) observational assessments whereby the teacher observes specific demonstration of skills, knowledge, or attitudes; and/or 3) performance assessments in which the teacher examines artifacts or student performances using specific assessment criteria.

Certified teachers (i.e., general educators and special educators) are responsible for designing assessments. Typically, certified teachers plan the methods of assessment when they are designing a unit of instruction. Paraprofessionals can assist with the implementation of the assessments under the direction of a certified teacher. For example, the paraprofessional can give a spelling test if the general education teacher has decided that a spelling test is the most appropriate way to determine if students can spell certain words. The teacher would model for the paraprofessional how to administer the spelling test. For instance, the teacher might show the paraprofessional how to say the word, use it in a sentence, and repeat the word. Some assessments, however, are not appropriate for paraprofessionals to administer. These include standardized assessment tools and certain informal inventories. As a team, identify those that are a part of your system.

Slightly different from assessment, evaluation is the process of interpreting and making judgments about assessment information. Assessment data alone have limited usefulness; they simply mirror the classroom instruction as it relates to students. The information gained through assessment becomes meaningful when it reflects something that is valued. For example, if a teacher values students' ability to problem solve, he or she might design two separate assessments. The first might be a traditional approach (i.e., paper and pencil) in which the students list the steps of a specific problem-solving process. The second assessment might be a demonstration of students' ability to apply those problem-solving skills to an actual dilemma. The teacher, not the paraprofessional, would use the assessment information from both items to evaluate whether each student has mastered the necessary skills of problem solving.

In evaluation, the teacher considers all of the assessment information and makes decisions on the basis of that information. The key evaluative question teachers ask themselves is "Are students learning what we want them to learn?" The answer to this question informs teachers about both the curriculum content and the instructional process. Often the answer helps excellent teachers adapt and modify their instruction to ensure that all students are reaching high standards. Typically, paraprofessionals do not have a significant role in evaluation procedures.

Questions 13–17 in Para Form 6: Up-Front Issues to Reach Consensus On highlight several assessment and evaluation issues for teams to consider. Although paraprofessionals do not maintain significant roles in assessment and evaluation, they do need to understand each classroom teacher's thoughts and practices on the topics so that they can be supportive.

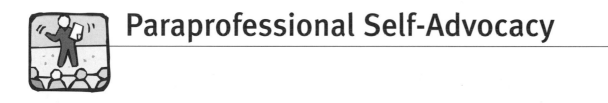

Paraprofessional Self-Advocacy

How Do I Ask for What I Need?

Asking for what one needs is an important skill, and it is particularly important for you as a paraprofessional. However, for a variety of reasons, it can be uncomfortable. Review Para Form 3: Advocacy Skills for Paraprofessionals: Asking for What You Need (located in the Para Forms appendix) and tie it directly to Para Form 6: Up-Front Issues to Reach Consensus On. The teacher should invite you to advocate for yourself by identifying the areas in which you need support or direction.

If you have not been told what assessment or work product should be generated during a particular lesson, use the steps outlined in Para Form 3: Advocacy Skills for Paraprofessionals to get clarification. You might say, "It is my understanding that Tom's goal in this lesson is to describe three new unit-related concepts and to initiate an interaction with a classmate. Is that accurate? What evidence or outcome do you expect him to generate?" Remember that the outcomes or products are important for both the general and special educator. This information should be directly related to the instructional decision making that these personnel are responsible for on an ongoing basis.

EFFECTS OF PARAPROFESSIONAL PROXIMITY

In most situations, children and youth act differently when adults are in close proximity to them. Lack of clarity about roles and responsibility can lead to excessive paraprofessional proximity. Giangreco, Edelman, Luiselli, and MacFarland (1997) identified eight challenges that result from the excessive proximity of paraprofessionals to students with disabilities:

- Interference with ownership and responsibility by general education teachers

- Separation from classmates

- Dependence on adults

- Limitation on peer interactions

- Limitation on receiving instruction from licensed teachers

- Loss of personal control

- Loss of gender identity

- Interference with the instruction of other students

As a team, discuss each of these challenges. What might each challenge look and sound like in your classroom or school? Perhaps your team could even obtain and read the article from which this information is taken (http://www.uvm.edu/~cdci/?Page=parasupport/chrono.html). Then list strategies you could employ to avoid each of the challenges. Generate several examples and solutions for each challenge, referring to Table 2.1 to guide the discussion.

To further explore this issue, team members might discuss the potential implications of each of the challenges. Put yourselves in the shoes of the student with a disability: How would you feel having an adult right next to you all day long? Clearly, the time children and youth spend together offers important opportunities for them to create mutual friendships and understanding. As adults, you must work hard to support those opportunities and then have the courage to step away to let them happen.

Table 2.1. Effects of paraprofessional proximity

Challenge	Example of the challenge	Example of how the challenge can be addressed
Interference with ownership and responsibility by general education teachers	When asked why a classroom teacher did not list the name of the student with disabilities alphabetically in his grade book, his response is, "Someone else is responsible for that student's assessment. I am responsible for the other 26 students in my class."	The general educator can include the names of all of the students in the classroom grade book. The paraprofessional can solicit the information from the appropriate team members and enter it in the grade book.
Separation from classmates	The paraprofessional sits with the student at the back of the room near the door. The special educator pulls the student out of the classroom for instruction.	The student can sit next to a peer in the middle of the row. The special educator can provide instruction in the classroom during reading time.
Student dependence on adults	The paraprofessional gathers and carries all of the student's materials to every class.	The paraprofessional can teach the student to use a picture schedule list (with materials) for each class. Peers can help the student gather and carry the materials.
Reduced student interaction with peers	The paraprofessional sits with the students at lunch.	The paraprofessional can supervise many students in the cafeteria without sitting at the students' table.
Limited instruction from licensed teachers	The paraprofessional designs and implements the majority of the instruction for the student with disabilities.	The team can implement collaborative teaching.
Loss of student's personal control	The paraprofessional makes all of the decisions (e.g., who the student works with, what color marker the student uses, when the student comes and goes in the classroom) for the student.	The student is taught how to make choices, and the adults respond to those choices.
Loss of gender identity	A female paraprofessional brings a male student into the women's restroom.	The team can identify a male staff member to help the student in the men's restroom. The school can designate one unisex restroom.
Interference with the instruction of other students	The paraprofessional is providing parallel instruction to the student with disabilities. When she is speaking to the student, classmates focus on her instead of the instruction being provided by the general educator.	The team can adapt the instruction (i.e., content and process) to facilitate the inclusion of the student with disabilities. The team can structure small-group work in which both adults are supervising and the learning outcomes for all students are clear.

Source: Giangreco, Edelman, Luiselli, and MacFarland (1997).

SELF-ADVOCATES' PERSPECTIVES ON PARAPROFESSIONAL PROXIMITY

Much of the professional literature on the effects of overreliance on paraprofessionals and of excessive proximity has focused on what researchers, teachers, and family members believe the person with disabilities might be thinking and experiencing. Broer, Doyle, and Giangreco (2005) asked 16 adults with moderate to severe disabilities to describe their public school experiences of having individual paraprofessional support in inclusive settings. Participants in this qualitative study identified the support they received from a paraprofessional as falling into four distinct categories: paraprofessional as friend, teacher, mother, and protector. Although, presumably, each of the educational teams in the lives of these young people had the best of intentions, the actual impact of paraprofessional proximity as described by the young people with disabilities was quite negative. The findings are presented briefly below. As a team, read each section and discuss the follow-up questions.

Paraprofessional as Friend

The participants in the study often described their only real "friends" as being paid paraprofessional staff. Often the paraprofessionals were the only people who were consistently kind, who spoke to them every day, and who were there to interpret what was happening in the school environment. Although on the surface this may appear to be fine, the long-term impacts have been devastating. First, of course, the paraprofessionals (like the teachers) were paid to be with the students. When the pay ceased, or for some other reason the paraprofessional left, the relationship ended. This should compel team members to be more deliberate in helping students understand the difference between being friendly and being a true friend. The second effect was that after years of public schooling, only one of the 16 study participants had a sustaining friendship that began in school. Others described lives of loneliness and isolation. As one person said, "I want to learn more about friends, like being a friend. But I can hardly do it if I have no friends." Another young person said, "I still can't understand why they just didn't want to have nothing to do with me" (Broer et al., 2005, p. 422).

Questions

1. In what ways can your team be certain to support students with disabilities in developing and maintaining friendships?
2. Why is this critical in everyone's life?
3. How will you demonstrate and clarify the differences between being friendly and being a friend?

Paraprofessional as Teacher

On the surface, "paraprofessional as teacher" may seem unproblematic; after all, paraprofessionals are supposed to help with instruction. Indeed, study participants made comments such as "She taught me a lot" and "He's a great guy." However, as discussed previously, many paraprofessionals' responsibilities now include providing direct instruction, yet they do not have the necessary training or support to do this effectively. Students in the study who had some of the most challenging learning characteristics were taught by personnel with the least amount of formal training. The young people shared the impact this experience had on their own perception of being valued as a student. One said, "They're [general education teachers] always telling me, 'We got too many kids in the classroom; we can't just deal with you.'" Another person shared, "They told me I couldn't get a teacher to help me because they're busy with other things in the classroom." And finally, "They can't really spend a lot of time with one person because they've got a class to teach" (Broer et al., 2005, p. 423).

Questions

1   What was the impact of these students' experiences on their own identities and feelings of value and worth as students?

2. Would it be okay for students without disabilities to have the same experiences?

Paraprofessional as Mother

Imagine what it would have felt like to have a mother figure with you at all times while in school. When paraprofessionals are completely responsible for a single student, they often take that responsibility very seriously. Based on a desire to perform their responsibilities well, the students in their charge are constantly under their watchful eyes. Now think about what that experience would be like if you were the student. As one student reported, "I was kind of getting embarrassed because I always had like a mother right there. People were like looking at me and stuff and saying, 'Why do you always have this person who is like twice as old as you?'" (Broer et al., 2005, p. 420). "I felt a little weird. I felt like I was like having a mother" (p. 421).

Questions

1. How would you have felt having your mother, or a mother figure, follow you around in school all day, every day?

2. Does the role of mother interfere with a student's ability to develop friendships in your class?

3. If the paraprofessional is acting in this manner (i.e., hovering too much), it is likely that he or she is not receiving enough direction and supervision. How can the classroom teacher and special educator change this experience?

Paraprofessional as Protector

Eleven of the sixteen young adults who were interviewed had been assigned paraprofessionals as protectors from students without disabilities who acted as bullies. Again, although at first glance this may appear to be a responsible thing to do, this solution did not address the student who acted as the bully. In essence, the victim (i.e., the student with a disability) became further isolated from the very people who could have been the most helpful: classmates. And the bully? The bully did not receive the supports and interventions that may have been needed to help him deal with his own issues and change his behavior. Sadly, one young adult has learned lessons that continue into his adulthood: "I mean you get picked on all of your life anyways, you can't really do much about it" (Broer et al., 2005, p. 423).

Questions

1. How does your team intervene with and support students who bully others?

2. How does your team work with students who are victims of bullying to support them and to broaden, rather than narrow, their circles of support?

Clearly, the students in the Broer et al. (2005) study have presented powerful information related to their firsthand experiences of having individual paraprofessional support. Although it cannot be assumed that all students with disabilities who receive support from paraprofessionals experience the same feelings and outcomes, it is clear that teams must listen and respond to the voices of young people. Of course, now comes the big question: How will you and your team respond to this information?

TEAM MEMBER COMMUNICATION

Most teachers engage in some sort of problem solving with members of the school community. This is particularly important when more than one adult (i.e., the general education teacher) is responsible for meeting students' needs. One way to streamline team problem solving is to develop a team meeting agenda that can predictably and efficiently move the team through the issues with a focus on solving the difficulty rather than simply talking about it. Para Form 7: Problem-Solving on the Fly, located in the Para Forms appendix, illustrates one format that your team might find helpful. If the teacher keeps this form in an accessible location, members of the team can fill it out between meetings. This approach ensures that the agenda is set and reviewed by team members prior to the meeting.

Reflection

- How common is it for any one team member to see others (i.e., peers, general education teachers) interacting with the student with disabilities?

- Does the student receive regular, ongoing instruction from the classroom teacher?

- Does the student with disabilities typically walk to and from classes with peers rather than with adults?

- What would it take to make these things happen?

- Would it be okay for students without disabilities to receive their primary instruction from paraprofessional staff? If not, why is it okay for students who have more complex learning challenges to do so?

- Does each member of the team experience the respect and regard of other team members?

CONCLUSION

The intention of this chapter is to give teachers and paraprofessionals the opportunity to plan how they will work together as a team. The questions in the text and on each worksheet can guide team members from the stage of getting to know one another to engaging in explicit conversations about each person's daily roles and responsibilities in the classroom. Chapter 3 shows team members how to become familiar with the learning characteristics of the students with disabilities whom they support during the year.

3

Supporting Individual Students

Objectives

- Learn ways to get to know students with disabilities
- Learn about IEPs
- Understand how to use an IEP
- Understand how to design and use individual student schedules

Throughout the school year, the educational team will learn a great deal about each student in the classroom. Among the most important aspects to understand about individual students with disabilities are their learning characteristics and priorities. Several sources of information can be especially helpful in these areas, including the following:

- Family vision statements
- Student profiles
- IEP matrixes
- Student learning priorities and supports

This chapter provides a brief description of each of these items and how these items can be used to gather and share information about students and their families.

HOW DO WE INCLUDE FAMILIES IN EDUCATIONAL PLANNING?

Without question, families are the cornerstone of educational planning. They are the people who know and love their child the most, and over time they will be the most consistent member of the educational team. Given these facts, other members of the team might find it very helpful to understand the hopes and dreams that a family has for the student. By listening to family members' dreams, knowledge, and experiences, teams are more likely to understand the parents' educational decision making.

The classroom teacher could invite the parents, student, special educator, and paraprofessional to a meeting to get to know and understand the family's vision. A clear message of welcome and collaboration is established when the classroom teacher, rather than the special educator, takes the initiative for this invitation. The meeting should be informal, positive, and nonjudgmental. The classroom teacher might send an invitation like the one shown in Figure 3.1.

You're Invited to an Afternoon Tea

Time: 1:00–3:00
Place: Mrs. Cleary's classroom, #245
Purpose: To listen to Mr. and Mrs. Whiteford and Andrew describe their dreams for Andrew's future. The intention is to understand the family's vision so we can all work together to take steps toward that vision.

Figure 3.1. Sample invitation for meeting with family to discuss the family's vision.

In preparation for the meeting, the classroom teacher would ask the parent(s) or caregiver(s) and student to look for a few photographs to bring to the meeting that reflect their experiences in the following areas of life:

- Favorite photographs of the student with the parent(s) or caregiver(s)
- The student at family/caregiver events (e.g., with siblings and cousins)
- Photographs in the neighborhood or community
- Photographs with friends and neighbors

If the parents or caregivers respond that the child or youth has no friends in the neighborhood, this would be very important information. The absence of such pictures should be a topic of discussion and, if important to the family, made a priority for the academic year.

The photographs could be a random collection or arranged in a mini-scrapbook, a small photo album, or a PowerPoint presentation prepared by the family. If the family needs support in preparing the materials, make yourself available to help. Two helpful resources for developing such materials are Doyle (2000) and Thompson, Meadan, Fansler, Alber, and Balogh (2007). Both articles provide structures related to communicating the essence of a person through pictures, words, and stories.

Once the materials are completed, invite the student and his or her parents to share their stories of membership and participation in each area mentioned previously. Your intention is to support the team in seeing and understanding this young person as a member of a family, neighborhood, school, and community. Some members of the team will be better able to understand the family's dreams or vision once they see the student as a member of various groups. If the student was included in general education classes the previous year, it is very helpful to share photos of that experience.

From this point, the classroom teacher or special educator should direct the conversation in a manner that supports the family, including the student, in constructing a family vision statement that becomes the core of all educational decision making. Here are several questions to consider when developing this statement:

- *How* do you want your child's school experience to be?
- *What* would make a good elementary, middle, or high school experience for your child?
- *Who* would you like your child to spend time with?
- *Where* would you like your child to spend time (e.g., playground, local hangout)?

These questions can easily be reworded for students:

- What do you want school to be like?
- Who do you want to spend time with?
- Do you want to hang out on the playground, at the pizza place, or somewhere else? Where else?
- Do you want to hang out with or without adults?

The next step would be for a member of the team to meet with the student and several peers to answer the question: What would it take to make these things happen?

Figure 3.2 highlights the Whitefords' family vision statement for their teenage son, Andrew. In this statement, family members clearly described the type of life they want for Andrew and how that connected directly with the learning priorities developed for him.

Another way to support the family in articulating the family's values is to utilize *Choosing Options and Accommodations for Children: A Guide to Educational Planning for Students with Disabilities, Second Edition* (COACH; Giangreco, Cloninger, & Iverson, 1998). Typically, the special educator facilitates the process outlined in the COACH manual. The process is rooted in a parent interview, during which parents are asked specific questions that lead the team to 1) understand the family's valued life outcomes and 2) develop the student's IEP goals and objectives for the year. If the preparation is done well, the entire process should take 1.5–2 hours. At the end of the 2 hours, the team will have identified IEP

A. Family value: *Andrew's life will be enhanced with the combination of conceptual and procedural knowledge.*

  1. We do know the importance of procedural knowledge as it applies to many different subject areas. Indeed, Andrew does benefit from being taught specific procedures.

  2. However, we do not want Andrew's world to be reduced to procedural knowledge. We want his curriculum to be a combination of procedural and conceptual learning. The conceptual learning allows him access to rich and interesting ideas, while the procedural knowledge gives him the skills to manipulate the information.

B. Family value: *Andrew will participate in general education classes.*

  1. We want Andrew to learn and retain some of the fundamental knowledge of the course.

  2. Our experience tells us that given the opportunity to learn new and interesting information, Andrew's curiosity is sparked and he is likely to continue that learning.

  3. We want him to acquire breadth and depth in content knowledge as a way to enrich his life and to provide him the knowledge-based experiences that he can connect with others.

  4. We want him to have high school experiences (e.g., group work, conversations, class projects) in classes that increase the opportunities to interact with peers.

C. Family value: *Andrew will participate in student groups and student projects.*

  1. We want Andrew to have friends; shared experiences (both in class and after school) increase the likelihood of that happening.

  2. We want him to have the support he needs to participate in and interpret social cues.

  3. We want to create the social bridges that he may need in order to develop friendships.

D. Family value: *We want Andrew's curiosity to continue to be a motivator for him.*

  1. Including Andrew with the appropriate supports and adaptations allows him to access the curriculum.

  2. Leveraging and expanding Andrew's skills related to technology will enable him to explore new information and to communicate that information to others.

E. Family value: *Andrew will have the self-management skills that he needs to move independently throughout his day.*

  1. Andrew has learned many ways to manage his own energy levels (e.g., body breaks, listening to music); we want him to make the decisions about when to use them.

We want the school to assist us in teaching Andrew certain skills related to independence as we generate them and as the need arises. For example, moving between classes independently or with peers is a high self-management priority. The skill set has aspects that require instruction and support. We would like the school personnel to teach him this skill. Nonexample: We don't need assistance with home activities (e.g., chores) at this point, but if we do at some point, we will request that support.

Figure 3.2. The Whiteford family's vision for Andrew's high school experience.

priorities that are directly linked to the family's valued life outcomes. Again, the key is for the team to understand the family's vision and values and how they align with the learning priorities for the academic year ahead.

Why does all of this matter? Once a child and family are humanized and their visions, hopes, and dreams are articulated, educational personnel are more likely to better understand the family's experience; understanding is the first step toward assisting the family in making their visions and dreams a reality. Because any given educational team is only on the journey for a short period of time, it is critical that the family hold on to their vision. Family members are simply inviting members of each team to assist them in their life's journey.

WHO IS THE STUDENT?

With a solid understanding of the family's vision and how that vision relates to the student's learning priorities, the team and family can share some fairly specific information about the student. Para Form 8: Student Profile (see Figure 3.3 for a filled-in example in this chapter, a blank version appears in the Para Forms appendix) provides information related to the student's learning style, motivators, and effective instructional strategies. Invite the student and family to add to and shape the information based on their experiences.

Once the form is completed, you might also find it helpful to attach a folder that contains the student's portfolio of work samples, photographs, tape recordings, and progress reports that exemplify some of the information on the Student Profile form. Becoming familiar with this background information saves team members valuable time in getting to know students with disabilities.

The team could review and discuss the student's profile and how this information might affect decisions related to classroom management and instruction. As the school year progresses, each member of your education team will discover additional characteristics about the student with disabilities and may want to update the student's profile accordingly. Many teams have found this type of information helpful at the end of the school year when assisting students with making the transition to the next grade. In some situations, teachers also use this form for students without disabilities.

WHY IS CLASSROOM PARTICIPATION IMPORTANT?

Participation in ordinary life events and activities provides the opportunity for connecting with others and building friendships. For children and youth, school provides the primary contextual meeting ground. Through engagement in shared classroom experiences over time, students with and without disabilities discover aspects of both the explicit and implicit curriculum. The classroom provides the context and activities that allows for all students to participate in a rich and interesting curriculum.

Para Form 8

Student Profile

Student: Shawn   Paraprofessional: Mr. Smith

Parents: Carol and Frank   General educator: Mrs. Townsend

Friends: Ken, Sara, Andrew   Special educator: Ms. Green

About the Student

1. What are this student's strengths?

   Shawn is a visual learner with a positive attitude. He is organized and is strong in his use of technology. Shawn is good at and enjoys basketball.

2. Over the past 6 months, in what areas has the student shown the most growth?

   Shawn has shown growth in the use of peer supports. Shawn now uses gestural prompts rather than verbal prompting.

3. What is the student's learning style? (circle one)

   (Visual-linguistic)   Auditory   Body-kinesthetic

   Musical-rhythmic   Interpersonal   Other

4. How does the student communicate? (circle as many as apply)

   Verbal   Gestural   Cued speech

   Sign language   Hand gestures   Letter or word board

   Facilitated communication   Objects   Head movements

   Objects   Pictures   Eye gaze

   Facial expressions   (Picture symbols)   Other:

5. Does the student need assistance with communication?   ☐ No   ☑ Yes

   Please describe: Sometimes people need to ask Shawn to repeat himself or to show a picture.

6. How do peers assist this student with communication?

   Peers will do this independently when in groups and when adults are not too close to Shawn.

Classroom Information

7. Describe the student's literacy skills or level.   Shawn is at a 1.5-2nd grade reading level.

   a. Picture reading: Yes

   b. Sight word recognition: Uses phonetic approaches

   c. Fluency: 15

   d. Comprehension: 18

   e. Favorite books: Animal or sports books

_____

(continued)

Para Form 8
(CONTINUED)

8. How does the student access written information? Shawn reads pictures with assistance of peer or paraprofessional.

   a. Same text as peers   He writes his idea onto a   b. Multilevel curriculum at the ___15___ reading level
   sticky note and places it on the picture in the textbook.
   c. Books on tape: yes   d. Other: Scanning programs with voice output.

9. What types of technology has the student used in the past?

   (Remote control devices)   Switches   Computer games (names)

   PowerPoint   Internet searching   (Inspiration)

   Kidspiration   Other software: Other hardware:

Peer Relationships

10. Who are the student's friends?   Ken, Sara, and Andrew

    a. What do they do during school together? Is this frequently prompted by an adult?

       They participate in school projects, eat lunch and study together. This is frequently prompted by an adult.

    b. What do they do after school or on weekends? Is this frequently prompted by an adult?

       They do not get together unless Shawn's mother organizes something.

Teaching Information

11. What do you do to leverage the student's strengths?

12. How do you facilitate the student's connection with peers?

    We put them in groups of 3-5 where everyone has a role. Typically the paraprofessional is not in the group.

13. How do you facilitate a sense of belonging and contribution on behalf of the student with disabilities?

    Everyone has responsibilities in the class. I speak to every student every day.

14. In the past, what specific instructional strategies have and have not been successful?

    Delayed responding and visuals work well. Long verbal directions do not work well.

15. If a paraprofessional will be involved in supporting this student, what are the expectations for him or her?

    The paraprofessional meets with the teachers twice a month to hear about upcoming curriculum for the class. The teachers will demonstrate any new instructional techniques at these meetings.

Summary

1. Increased efforts around social relationships. We can do this by having Shawn participate in an afterschool or community service club. This may also foster interdependence as all members of the club will be working together to complete community service activities for others.

2. Increased instructional efforts to access and create appropriate adaptations for reading in the content area. Perhaps using an online flashcard program would help with word recognition and meaning.

Based on this conversation, what areas need to be addressed this year?

Figure 3.3.   Example of Para Form 8: Student Profile.

To design appropriate supports (e.g., material supports or personnel supports) for student participation in the classroom, the team must understand the student's engagement with peers during academic and nonacademic times. Para Form 9: Participation in Daily Classroom Routines (found in the Para Forms appendix) can be used to note a student's classroom participation and relationship skills. Once the supports are designed, teachers can model them for the paraprofessional as well.

WHAT IS AN INDIVIDUALIZED EDUCATION PROGRAM?

Every student receiving special education services has an IEP. The IEP contains documentation of the student's learning priorities for the current school year. These learning priorities are stated as annual goals and short-term objectives. The IEP is developed each year by the student's education team, which consists of personnel from his or her school (e.g., school administrator, special and general educators, school psychologist), the student's parents or caregivers, and possibly the student and his or her friends. Some students require additional personnel support in order to benefit from special education, as stipulated in IDEA of 1990 (PL 101-476). These supports are referred to in IDEA as "related services personnel" and include speech-language pathologists, occupational therapists, physical therapists, and vision therapists. The specific related services personnel required by an individual student are identified on his or her IEP.

As a member of the student's IEP team, paraprofessionals may be invited to participate in the student's IEP meetings. Paraprofessionals can provide important and necessary information about supporting the student with disabilities. In such cases, it is helpful if the classroom teacher or special educator takes the time to prepare the paraprofessional for the meeting. The paraprofessional should understand the purpose and function of the meeting, as well as her or his specific role during it. Ideally, the teacher would ask the paraprofessional ahead of time to jot down a few thoughts about one or more agenda items to share at the meeting.

Each member of the IEP team should be clear about the student's learning goals and objectives. The team should work together to create one set of unified learning priorities and objectives for the student. Individual team members should not have their own goals and objectives. For example, it would be inappropriate to have a set of goals for speech therapy, a set for occupational therapy, and a set for special education. There should be one set of educational goals for the student with documentation of how the special educator and, when appropriate, related services personnel will support the student in attaining his or her goals. The IEP document must include an account of the following:

- What can the student do at the present time?
- What is considered most important for the student to learn this year?
- What specialized instruction does the student require in order to accomplish these learning goals?
- Who are the education team members who share responsibility for implementing the IEP?
- How will the student's progress be measured and documented?

When your educational team is providing support to a student who has an IEP, it is important for each member of the team to have a working knowledge of the individual student's learning priorities and how to support the student in reaching his or her learning goals. Typically, the special educator reviews the student's learning priorities with the general educator and the paraprofessional and then demonstrates how each member of the team will support the student in accomplishing those learning priorities. During these training opportunities, the team should develop strategies for supporting the student with disabilities that involve a variety of educators and other personnel, not just the paraprofessional. Creating a useful IEP is a critical aspect of instructional design, as it enables the team to work together so that the student with disabilities and the paraprofessional do not become overdependent on each other.

Overdependence on paraprofessionals has emerged in current research as problematic (Giangreco, Broer, & Edelman, 1999; Giangreco et al., 1997). If a member of the team suspects that an overdependence is emerging between the student and the paraprofessional (or any member of the team), the team must address this in their instructional programming for the student. Overdependence can be a sign of lack of clarity regarding the adult's (often the paraprofessional's) role and/or the learning priorities for the student. Because it is not the paraprofessional's responsibility to set the student's learning priorities, a lack of clarity regarding the learning priorities or the roles of educational team members in helping the student to accomplish these priorities must be addressed by team members immediately.

As a team, take time to review the IEPs of the students in your class to ensure that your entire education team has a shared understanding of each student's individualized learning priorities. Be certain to ask any questions that will increase your understanding of the student's learning priorities. The special education teacher or classroom teacher should check for understanding with the paraprofessional. It is important to remember that IEPs are confidential documents; any information contained in them may not be shared with other paraprofessionals, teachers, students, parents, or community members outside of the student's specific education team.

HOW DOES THE PARAPROFESSIONAL USE AN INDIVIDUALIZED EDUCATION PROGRAM?

Paraprofessionals need to use information from students' IEPs every day. However, in some situations, IEP documents do not lend themselves to portability and use on a daily basis. Therefore, if the special educator has not already done so, this is a good time for the team to transfer relevant information that the teacher and paraprofessional will need from the IEP documents to a more useable format. Two such formats can be found on Para Form 10: Individualized Education Program Matrix and Para Form 11: Student Learning Priorities and Support worksheets (see Figures 3.4 and 3.5 for filled-in examples in this chapter; blank versions of these forms appear in the Para Forms appendix). Both of these worksheets serve multiple functions, such as tracking students' learning priorities and necessary support, daily class schedule, and daily support schedule. As a team, talk about which format would be more helpful for your team, or design your own based on your needs.

PARA FORM 11

Student Learning Priorities and Support

Directions: In the left-hand column, check whether you will use a multilevel approach or a curriculum overlapping approach. Then, list the student's learning priorities that need to be addressed during the day and in a specific class. In the center and right-hand columns, list the instructional strategy and check the supports (people and/or materials) that are necessary for the student to accomplish his or her learning priorities.

Student: _Katie_

General educator: _Mrs. Peters_

Special educator: _Mr. Henry_

Paraprofessional: _Mr. Daniels_

Learning priorities (What)	Instructional strategy (How)	Support (People and/or materials)
Learning priorities for the day ☐ Curriculum overlapping ☐ Multilevel instruction • Participate during each class • Bring necessary materials • Move to and from classes with peers • Curriculum overlapping	Same as peers	People: ☐ Friends ☑ Classroom teacher ☐ Special educator ☐ Paraprofessional Materials: To be determined
Learning priorities for _reading_ class ☐ Curriculum overlapping ☑ Multilevel instruction • Listen to stories with the whole class • Choose a book from the library and check it out • Use a switch to activate a taped story	Same as peers; limit book choices by topic (animals or sports)	People: ☐ Friends ☑ Classroom teacher ☐ Special educator ☑ Paraprofessional Materials: Big Red switch, tape recorder, tape
Learning priorities for _science_ class ☐ Curriculum overlapping ☑ Multilevel instruction • Participate in experiments • Learn two concepts per unit	Same as peers; peers assist with experiment, ask same questions but, with two-choice cards for answers	People: ☑ Friends ☑ Classroom teacher ☐ Special educator ☑ Paraprofessional Materials: To be determined

The Paraprofessional's Guide to the Inclusive Classroom: Working as a Team
Copyright © 2008 by Mary Beth Doyle. All rights reserved.
Available through Brookes Publishing Co., Baltimore, 1-800-638-3775, www.brookespublishing.com

Figure 3.5. Example of Para Form 11: Student Learning Priorities and Support.

PARA FORM 10

Individualized Education Program Matrix

Directions: List the student's daily activities or class periods across the top row. Then list a student's learning priorities in the left-hand column. Place a check in each of the corresponding boxes in which each learning priority will be addressed throughout the school day.

Student: _Josh_ Grade: _5_

General educator: _Mrs. Jones_

Special educator: _Mrs. Peters_

Paraprofessional: _Ms. Smith_

Individualized education program goals	Reading	Science	Gym	Snack	Math	Lunch and recess	Spelling	Computer science (lab)
Makes a choice between two options	X	X	X		X		X	
Indicates "more"	X	X	X	X	X		X	X
Active in leisure time with peers				X			X	
Activates Big Red switch		X				X		X
Uses calculator to check calculations						X	X	X

From Giangreco, M.F., Cloninger, C.J., & Iverson, V.S. (1998). *Choosing outcomes and accommodations for children (COACH): A guide to educational planning for students with disabilities* (2nd ed.). Baltimore: Paul H. Brookes Publishing Co.; adapted by permission.

In *The Paraprofessional's Guide to the Inclusive Classroom: Working as a Team* by Mary Beth Doyle (2008).

Figure 3.4. Example of Para Form 10: Individualized Education Program Matrix.

As your education team transfers the information that paraprofessionals will need from the IEP document to a more useable format, it is critical that the paraprofessional understand the information as it is written. The team should be careful not to use jargon.

Paraprofessional Self-Advocacy

The general educator, the special educator, and you as the paraprofessional all need to understand each student's learning priorities. In addition, each member of the education team needs to specifically understand your role and responsibilities in supporting the student with disabilities to move toward accomplishment of his or her learning priorities.

You should review Para Form 10: Individualized Education Program Matrix or Para Form 11: Student Learning Priorities and Support that the team has completed. Explain your understanding of the student's instructional priorities and ask the special educator for any necessary clarification. Also ask the special and general educators when and how you will receive direction about how you should support the student in each area. Typically, you will be given lesson or activity plans and will observe modeling of specialized instruction and data collection.

It is also important that your role and responsibilities in relation to the delivery of instruction be clear. One strategy for accomplishing this is to have your education team discuss the following questions:

- What is my role in supporting the special educator and the general educator to ensure that the student with disabilities is able to accomplish his or her learning priorities?

- How will I support the student with disabilities—without being too intrusive—in accomplishing each of the student's learning priorities during class?

- When will other team members support the student with disabilities in the inclusive classroom in moving toward his or her IEP goals?

- Does the student with disabilities need specific adaptations to move toward accomplishing his or her learning priorities? If so, what is my role in developing and implementing these adaptations?

WHY ARE STUDENT SCHEDULES IMPORTANT?

Each member of your education team will need to be familiar with every student's daily schedule. Although schedules may change or be modified over time, it is helpful for education personnel to know where the students with disabilities are throughout the school day.

If the general and special educators have already completed a schedule for each student, your team should refer to that schedule. If the general and special educators have not completed student schedules, refer to Para Form 10: Individualized Education Program Matrix or Para Form 11: Student Learning Priorities and Support form as a guideline for doing so. Keep in mind that if your team fills out these worksheets in the chronological order of the student's day, the daily schedule will be listed in order.

Who is responsible for the student's schedule? Increasingly, team members are teaching students to manage and follow their own personal schedules. Learning to arrange one's daily activities and to manage the multiple transitions necessary throughout the day are important life skills in the area of personal management. On the basis of each student's individual strengths and needs, the classroom teacher or special educator can develop a schedule format that is most appropriate. There are any number of creative formats the schedules can take, including photographs of daily activities, picture symbols, objects, and Braille.

After a certified member of the team has designed the student's individual schedule, he or she needs to train other members on the team, including the paraprofessional, in how to teach the student to use the schedule. The specific instructional strategy chosen must match the student's learning characteristics and needs. For example, a student with moderate intellectual disabilities might require a gestural prompt toward a picture schedule to remind the student to gather the appropriate materials for the next class. Another student with similar characteristics might need delayed responding techniques. Typically, the special education teacher will identify this strategy. Instructional consistency across people will increase the likelihood that the student will learn the skill set.

ACTIVITY 7

Who Is Peter?

Peter is a young man who received one-to-one paraprofessional support from first grade through 21 years of age. At 22 years of age, Peter enrolled at Trinity College of Vermont through the audit option, which enabled him to take typical college classes without earning credits. Utilizing the audit option gave college personnel maximum flexibility to adapt and modify course content. Peter was eager to learn how to be a college student, which to him meant acting "cool" and learning "important stuff." Peter was articulate, thoughtful, and friendly. He learned quickly, was persistent, and had a good memory. He could not read or write, but he was able to dictate his thoughts to others so that they could be written down. The essay shown in the following case study was the outcome of a 6-month process of dictation. Peter's dictations were typed by another person, who also inserted punctuation to reflect his pacing and inflection. After each section was written, the typist reread the section to Peter so he could edit the essay with regard to the sound and pacing.

Take a few minutes to read Peter's story. Then, as a team, discuss the following questions:

1. Who is Peter? What school experiences contributed to or detracted from his growth as a young man?

2. What was the impact of paraprofessional support on Peter's educational career?

3. What was the relationship between Peter and his teachers and paraprofessionals? When Peter described the difficulties of "always having someone on my back" (i.e., paraprofessionals), do you think this was an issue with Peter's paraprofessional?

4. How is Peter's experience similar to situations you have encountered? How would your team handle a situation like this?

5. What has Peter taught your team? What could your team do differently with the students you currently work with?

Think about the impact that special education services had on Peter's life. Peter's insights should encourage your team to consider all of the needs of a student and to plan supports that are minimally intrusive.

I'm Not Special Ed. Anymore: My Name Is Peter[1]
By Peter Hunton

I'm a tall, handsome, single guy. I'm 22 years old. I am a college student, and I'm not a special ed. student anymore. I like playing basketball. I like exercising. I like hanging out in downtown Burlington. I like being with my friends. I like jazz and rock-and-roll music. I like school, too, because now I am taking very interesting classes. I especially love my History of the '60s class. I've gotten more out of that class than out of any other class that I have ever taken. I never liked any other class before. I like that class because the teacher has a sense of humor and teaches a lot of stuff. She teaches about women, the Vietnam War, and the Civil Rights movement. It's all really powerful stuff. The class is busy and outgoing.

I don't like boring teachers. Boring teachers teach slowly and don't have a sense of humor. I had a lot of boring teachers in high school because I was special ed. In high school, if you're special ed., they make you do stupid stuff like brushing your teeth in school. That's not good because that's stuff you do in kindergarten. They also give you stupid kindergarten contracts when you're in special ed. in high school.

I was in high school for 6 years. That's a long time to be in a place you don't like. In my high school, they always had someone on my back. The person was a tour guide. There was always a teacher or an aide hanging on my back like I was a baby. Now I don't have people hanging on my back because I'm not a special ed. kid anymore.

[1]*From* Hunton, P., & Doyle, M.B. (1999). I'm not special ed. anymore: My name is Peter. *The Association for Persons with Severe Handicaps Newsletter, 25*(10), 22; reprinted by permission.

I couldn't do sports or anything in high school. I wasn't in any clubs because I didn't have any friends. I hated being special ed. because when people talk to me they talked to me like a baby. They talk very slow and loud, as if I were deaf. I wish they would have talked to me like they did the other kids. They talk to them like adults.

I hated being special ed. because I didn't have any friends. Now I dream about having friends. I'm not special ed., so I can make friends now. People take me seriously now. Now I'm not special ed., and I have a friend whose name is Chuck. Chuck goes to college, too. We exercise and play basketball together.

I'm not special ed. anymore. My name is Peter. I'm a college student. I like college because it is open and people like to talk to you. The other kids don't care if you were special ed. in high school. I'm a lot happier now because I have friends. Mostly the other college kids don't treat me like a baby. But sometimes the college professors do treat me like a 10-year-old kid. Maybe it's because the professors never grew up with special ed. kids. They grew up in the 1960s and then special ed. kids were put away.

I learn a lot more stuff now, too. I get to learn stuff I never learned before. The most important things that I learned this year are how to speak more clearly and to share my ideas. I've also learned how to joke around with people. I'm really liking college. Now people call me by my name; they don't call me names. My name is Peter, and I am not a special ed. kid anymore!

CONCLUSION

Throughout this chapter, team members have had the opportunity—through activities, discussions, and worksheets—to become familiar with the students with disabilities with whom they are working. Hopefully, each team member has a good picture of each student's strengths, needs, and preferred learning mode. The team should have agreed on the format that will be used to ensure clear communication about how, when, and where each student's IEP goals will be addressed throughout the school day. Chapter 4 shows team members how to design the specialized instructional techniques and strategies that will ensure consistency of instruction.

4

Providing Curricular and Individualized Instructional Support

Objectives

- Articulate role and job expectations
- Define *multilevel curriculum and instruction* and *curriculum overlapping*
- Distinguish between learning outcomes and general supports
- Explain the function of preteaching techniques
- Describe the common components of daily routines
- Explain the principle of partial participation
- Describe how to provide instructional prompts
- Explain how to use curricular adaptations
- Describe delayed responding techniques
- Describe note-taking strategies

Typically, the first challenge for team members when identifying curricular priorities for individual students is agreeing on what constitutes an *appropriate curriculum*. Team members may find themselves disagreeing on the balance between functional and academic curriculum, how much time students should spend on campus versus off campus, and how much time they should spend in general education classes versus special education classes. In many cases, however, team members are debating the wrong issues.

WHAT ARE OUR TEAM'S EXPECTATIONS FOR STUDENTS?

Prior to engaging in group conversations about curricular priorities, it is helpful for team members to reflect on their own underlying assumptions and expectations about curriculum content for students with disabilities. Parents, teachers, school personnel, and community members all have a set of biases that have a direct impact on their thoughts about what is and is not important for all students. It is critical that each member of your team identify his or her own biases, acknowledge and discuss these biases with others on the team, and discuss the potential impact of differing perspectives on the educational program for each student. Seek to understand the perspectives of others and to find points of intersection and challenge. When the points of disagreement are identified, avoid becoming defensive or trying to persuade others to agree with your point of view; rather, remain open to the person with whom you disagree. Ask, "I hear what you're saying, but I haven't thought about it that way. Could you tell me more?" Give the person more time to explain his or her point of view.

As a team, practice this by reading and discussing the perspectives of the Cunningham family, who describe their expectations for their son, Kurt (see Figure 4.1). The Cunninghams have developed a family vision that guides their educational decision making. Kurt attends middle school in Michigan and has Williams syndrome. The Cunningham family express their beliefs in a clear and explicit manner. They want Kurt included in general education classes and activities. They value the knowledge, skills, and abilities that he will learn alongside his peers without disabilities. Their clarity on the balance of academic content and functional curriculum is stated in a manner that leaves no room for misunderstanding. Their values are easily translated for the teachers and related services personnel who are responsible for designing and implementing daily instruction that aligns with Kurt's IEP goals and objectives within an inclusive community.

Certainly, challenges may arise when some members of the team do not share the value of inclusive education or have not had the opportunity to teach in an inclusive situation. These members may make comments such as "Kids like Kurt shouldn't be learning about the Industrial Revolution; they should be learning how to grocery shop" or "It's more important for kids like Kurt to be learning job skills and how to balance a checkbook." Depending on the lens through which various team members see Kurt, both the suggested educational input and possible outcomes may be very different. Through the Cunninghams' lens, rich and interesting curriculum content, knowledge, and experiences provide critical learning opportunities for Kurt both at present and in the future, and these learning opportunities are in fact functional. In this situation, the team might respond with a question such as, "In

We are firm believers in the power of knowledge and the importance of being a well-rounded person. It is our desire that Kurt have opportunities to learn a variety of age-appropriate subject matter for the attaining of skills as well as for pure enjoyment. We hope that he will be inspired by the novels, poems, science experiments, history lessons, art, and music that he experiences throughout his educational journey.

Although Kurt is unable to demonstrate proficiency comparable to that of his peers, it is important to us that Kurt continue to participate in the learning experiences that unfold each day in his various classes. We have readily observed that this has expanded his frame of reference and has helped him more fully engage and be a member of society, since he has had opportunities to learn information that is common to the everyday person.

We believe that being in classes with typical peers has, and will continue to, yield Kurt opportunities to learn important life skills, such as the importance of being on time (to class or by handing in an assignment), the importance of studying, and the importance of paying attention—all of which are important skills that will translate into job skills for Kurt. We also found that opportunities to attain functional job skills are embedded in various classwork and homework assignments. It is our desire that Kurt continue to have these types of opportunities and continue to have peers to model this behavior and assist him in his attempts.

Figure 4.1. The Cunningham family vision.

what ways would we need to adapt and accommodate curriculum and instruction in order to meet Kurt's learning priorities in social studies class?" A very different lens would focus on curriculum priorities, such as daily life skills and prevocational work.

The general education curriculum provides all students with many opportunities to explore the world around them. Classroom teachers design interesting units of instruction and embed skill development with the intent of helping all students to discover interests, passions, and ways to contribute to the community and society. Ethically, how can school personnel continue to exclude the most vulnerable members of the community from these experiences? Imagine if they focused on sparking the fires of intellectual curiosity in students with disabilities. The lives and experiences of all students would be enriched as, together, they engaged in the world around them.

Take a moment and have the classroom teachers on your team write down the major topics they will be teaching over the next month. Next, list the enduring understandings the team members hope to teach all of the students. For example, if you want students to really understand the contributions of American heroines during the Civil War, you might highlight the life of Sojourner Truth. Have students research her life, describing in detail Truth's contributions to freedom and to the women's rights movement. Some students will be able to describe several of her key contributions. Others will hear about these contributions but focus on being able to identify her photograph. Why does this matter? Why might this even be considered *functional?* Recognizing the photographs of such people as Sojourner Truth; Mahatma Ghandi; Martin Luther King, Jr.; John F. Kennedy; and others gives people with and without disabilities information with which to engage in conversations where meaningful connections can occur. Such recognition contributes to a common knowledge base and experience that makes students' lives—both now and in the future—rich and interesting.

Perhaps the explicit curriculum content is not the focus for a student with the most severe disabilities. However, such content does provide the context within which the student can learn other important skills that have been identified on his or her IEP, such as interacting with peers or using an augmentative communication device. During the unit on American heroines during the Civil War, the teacher may also go well beyond the facts to embody Sojourner Truth's beliefs in the worthiness and contributions of African American men and women. These beliefs could be realized right in the classroom, in the attitudes and behaviors surrounding the education of students with disabilities.

Reflection

What lens am I using when I think about the curriculum priorities for individual students?

What lens have I used with past students? What has been the long-term impact of this perspective on the lives of those students?

Where are those students now? Are they living lives (e.g., living, working, playing) that I would be happy to live?

One way to identify the curriculum priorities for students with moderate or severe disabilities is through the use of COACH (Giangreco et al., 1998) (see Chapter 3 for a description of COACH). When using COACH, all team members will clearly understand an individual's students learning priorities throughout the day. It is critical that the special education teacher take the lead role in the COACH process by becoming very familiar with it prior to inviting the family to participate.

WHAT ARE OUR TEAM'S ROLE EXPECTATIONS?

The focus of this book is not on the identification of curriculum priorities, but on the step *after* IEP goals have been identified: implementation within an inclusive context. Initially, it can be challenging to coordinate the adults in a classroom because the adults have very distinct roles and responsibilities. This section offers ways to accomplish this implementation that align with the law and personnel roles. The general educator and the special educator maintain primary responsibility for designing, developing, assessing, and evaluating daily instruction for all students in the classroom, including students with disabilities; paraprofessionals are responsible for supporting daily instruction and assisting with general classroom management. As mentioned in a previous chapter, paraprofessionals are never responsible for designing instruction, selecting instructional strategies, identifying instructional supports and accommodations, or conducting evaluations. They are also not responsible for designing feeding programs, making physical supports decisions (e.g., physical management and positioning), or designing communication systems. Clearly, these are the primary responsibilities of teachers and related services personnel.

Reflection

Think of your team right now.

- What is the paraprofessional's role with regard to instructional decisions?

- Who actually makes decisions, writes plans, and models instructional practices for the paraprofessional?

- Ask the paraprofessional if his or her experiences match the practices you have identified.

This discussion of roles is not meant to leave the paraprofessional out of the process of teaching and learning. Indeed, students benefit from the creative energy of every team member. Paraprofessionals can be invited to provide input, generate ideas, and assist in the development of materials and adaptations for students. However, licensed personnel must assume their responsibilities in relationship to students with disabilities. Sometimes, for a variety of reasons, paraprofessionals do have to make on-the-spot decisions about an adaptation that is not working or shift priorities based on a change in the classroom schedule. However, such on-the-spot decisions should not be the norm because then the entire point of receiving specialized instruction is lost.

More predictably for the paraprofessional and the student, the paraprofessional might be asked to provide certain types of support to individual students with disabilities, such as implementing specific instructional procedures developed by the special educator, assisting with physical management and positioning of the student as specified by the physical therapist, or using a specific feeding program designed by the occupational therapist. The paraprofessional also might be asked to assist individual students or small groups of students to review or practice skills under the direction of the general educator or the special educator. The key in all of these situations is that licensed staff design the programs first and provide direction, support, and training to the paraprofessional in a manner that enables him or her to assist with implementation.

A Paraprofessional's Reflection

My job has really changed over the last few years. I went from not receiving much ongoing support or direction from teachers to receiving a lot of very specific instruc-

tion. I didn't like it at first because I thought that meant the teachers didn't trust me. Then a teacher said to me, "Actually, we're providing direction and training so that you can do the job you are paid to do, and not my job!"

Now my job in the classroom involves organizing materials for learning stations, copying, entering information into the computer, and implementing lesson plans with individual students or small groups that have been designed by one of the teachers. I have a lot more variety, and because they show me how to help with the instruction, I actually feel a lot more confident. Now my team uses a four-step process that we follow for all new instructional plans written for students with disabilities (see Figure 4.2).

First, the special educator designs a formal instructional plan based on the student's IEP and classroom activities. Second, she shows me how the classroom teacher and I are supposed to implement the plan. After we are sure we know how to implement the plan, the third step is to decide who will provide the instruction and on which days and what it will look like. During this phase, we talk about my role, too. We are really clear about which students I will be helping and what that help will look like. Our final step is to review how the actual teaching is progressing. During this step, we look at the student's work and talk about how he or she is progressing toward the learning objectives. If the student isn't doing well, we make changes in the instructional plan at this point because we believe that if the student isn't learning well, we're probably not teaching well. These four steps are very important to my team because we avoid the common problem of having me be responsible for everything for the students with disabilities.

In my situation, my teachers have become my coaches! This certainly makes my job easier, and when the teachers do my annual evaluation, there is something to base

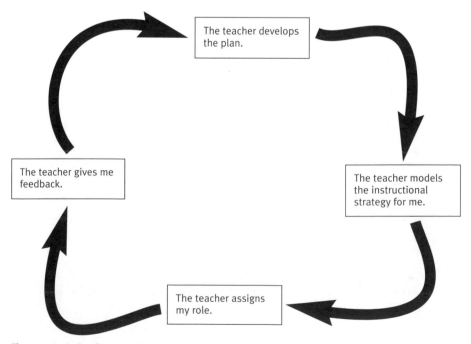

Figure 4.2. Cycle of support for paraprofessionals.

it on. I am lucky to work with teachers who take their roles and responsibilities very seriously while respecting my role as a paraprofessional.

CHARACTERISTICS OF EFFECTIVE PARAPROFESSIONAL SUPPORT

Over the past several years, there has been a substantial increase in the amount of research conducted on the use of paraprofessional support. Indeed, Giangreco's web site (http://www.uvm.edu/~cdci/parasupport) hosts dozens of abstracts and full-text articles, chapters, and program descriptions on the topic of paraprofessionals in schools. A review of this information leads to several key questions that your team might discuss:

1. Should students with the most complex learning challenges receive primary instruction from the least trained school staff?

2. Would it be okay for students without disabilities to spend a majority of their instructional time with paraprofessional staff? If it would be okay, why isn't it happening?

3. What evidence is there to support the current model of using paraprofessionals to support students with disabilities? Is this model effective?

Causton-Theoharis, Giangreco, Doyle, and Vadasy (2007) suggested that at least five elements are associated with the successful use of paraprofessionals to improve student outcomes:

1. The paraprofessional provides supplementary instruction, not primary instruction.

    *   *Practical application:* The teacher designs a unit and highlights how the student's individualized educational needs will be addressed within the unit. Teachers make decisions about grouping students and the appropriate utilization of classroom personnel, including volunteers, related service providers, and paraprofessionals.

2. Instruction is designed in a manner that does not require significant instructional decision making by the paraprofessional.

    *   *Practical application:* The teacher decides which instructional strategy is most appropriate, identifies the evidence or product the student will generate as a means of demonstrating learning, chooses the method of evaluation, and outlines the instructional grouping arrangements that will allow the student with disabilities to engage with peers. This last decision is key, as it is important that the paraprofessional and the student with disabilities are not isolated from the rest of the class. Deliberate decisions are made to support the paraprofessional in not hovering around the student with disabilities.

3. Proven instructional methods (i.e., research-based methods) are used.

    *   *Practical application:* The instructional strategy or approach that is used is rooted in research. The classroom teacher or special educator is responsible for making the decision about which approach or combination of approaches to use. This is where specialized instruction is highlighted.

4. Paraprofessionals are trained in the instructional approach and/or program that they are expected to implement.

    *   *Practical application:* Either the teacher or special educator teaches the paraprofessional how to use the instructional approach. This may include modeling the specific strategies that will be used.

5. Paraprofessionals are supervised and monitored to ensure consistency of instruction.

    *   *Practical application:* The teacher or special educator provides specific feedback to the paraprofessional on the latter's use of the strategies that have been modeled for him or her.

As your team continues reading this chapter, keep these five statements in mind. If paraprofessionals are really going to support instructional teams, they need to be used wisely and under the supervision of licensed personnel. You can use Para Form 12: Effective Utilization of Paraprofessional Support (located in the Para Forms appendix) to assess how well your team is applying these five elements.

I cannot emphasize enough that teachers must make the decisions regarding the types of supports that the paraprofessional will be providing to students in the classroom. In general, the supports should improve teachers' abilities to meet the educational needs of all of the students in the class, including the student(s) with disabilities.

WHAT ARE MULTILEVEL CURRICULUM AND INSTRUCTION AND CURRICULUM OVERLAPPING?

Multilevel curriculum and instruction and *curriculum overlapping* are two very important concepts for all team members to understand (e.g., parents, classroom teachers, paraprofessionals, related services providers). These concepts are especially important when supporting students with disabilities in general education settings.

Multilevel Curriculum and Instruction

Multilevel curriculum and instruction is an approach to teaching that has been used in classrooms for a very long time. It refers to teaching "a diverse group of students within a shared activity in which students have individually appropriate learning outcomes in the same curriculum area" (Giangreco, Cloninger, & Iverson, 1998, pp. 11–12). Multigraded classrooms provide a clear example of this concept.

Components of Multilevel Curriculum and Instruction

Multilevel curriculum and instruction has four key components (Campbell et al., 1988; Giangreco & Putnam, 1991):

1. "Diverse group of learners" refers to the classroom composition reflecting the natural diversity within the community.

- *Practical application:* A seventh-grade classroom has students who reflect the diversity in the community, including ability, race, and socioeconomic variations.

2. "Shared activity" refers to all students' participation in the same activity.

   - *Practical application:* During a social studies lesson on state geography, all students, readers and nonreaders alike, participate with reading materials that match their instructional levels. The materials range from pictures to advanced written text.

3. Students have "individually appropriate learning outcomes" within the context of the activity, meaning that the outcomes will be different for some students.

   - *Practical application:* Two students are expected to make connections between the political issues in their state and issues related to the federal government; another student with severe disabilities will learn to identify his state on a map using a match-to-sample strategy. Match-to-sample is an instructional strategy that entails the student matching two similar items. In this example, the student might match a card that has a picture of his state with a map of the United States. Some students might make connections between their local communities and the state government; still others among classroom issues and the student government of the school.

4. Students are being instructed in the same curriculum area.

   - *Practical application:* All students in the classroom are studying social studies and, in particular, state geography.

All four of these elements are in place continuously within the context of multilevel curriculum and instruction. Multilevel curriculum and instruction assumes that students are engaging in the same activity while pursuing related learning outcomes at different levels.

Language and Literacy Levels in Multilevel Curriculum

When using multilevel curriculum and instruction, it is critical that a member of the team, often the special educator or speech-language pathologist, continually pay attention to the language and literacy demands of lessons. For every curriculum topic there must be materials that are accessible for all students in the classroom. Increasingly, high-interest and low-readability texts are available. Given the diversity within classrooms today, teams should expect to find materials ranging from pictures to complex written texts. It is common for elementary teachers to have this range available for students; middle and high school teachers should pay attention to this issue as well. Table 4.1 highlights several web sites as places to start to explore high-interest, low-readability texts and text sets.

A second practical support that can help expand language for all students is the use of online flashcards that are accessed both in school and from home. Many such programs are available online; simply search for the phrase *online flashcards* (http://www.flashcard exchange.com is one site). Teams should consider the needs of students at all levels when purchasing such programs. For instance, find a program that allows for the use of pictures as well as words. The flashcard program itself can also become a system of communication between home and school. If parents and other team members access the program, they

Table 4.1. High-interest, low-readability online resources

Helpful search terms: *Hi Lo; ESL readers;* photo essays of the topic; *high-interest, low-readability*

http://www.kidsinbetween.com: Publishes and distributes educational materials that cover all curriculum areas. The materials are written for older students who read below grade level. Many of the texts are written at the 4.0 reading level.

http://www.academictherapy.com: High Noon Books, a division of Academic Therapy Publications, focuses on books for students who read at significantly lower reading levels than their peers.

http://www.resourceroom.net/older/hilow_sources.asp: Highlights several additional web sites related to this topic.

http://childrensbooks.about.com/od/toppicks/tp/hi_lo_books.htm: Lists several additional related sites for teachers.

will have a better understanding of what has been prioritized for the student at school. Parents of younger students might play the games embedded within the program with their children, while parents of older students might use the information to engage in conversations at the dinner table or while driving to and from places. Speech-language pathologists can use the flashcard vocabulary to design interventions that support the student's functional communication needs in the classroom. In high school, where a student has several teachers and support personnel, team access of flashcards allows all team members to work with the student on the same skill sets.

A third way to support students' language needs is to maximize the use of your word processing program. For example, Microsoft Word and Adobe Acrobat Reader have text-to-speech options. Microsoft Word also has a readability function to calculate the readability level of word documents. These functions improve the teacher's ability to support students in accessing written language. Contact your school's information technology professional for help in accessing these options if you need assistance.

When teams have a better idea of the tools that are easily available for supporting students with disabilities, they often more readily move forward in including those students. Ultimately, teachers learn that instructional approaches, strategies, and adaptations that are necessary for some students can actually help all students (see Table 4.2 for an example of an instructional support plan that includes various instructional goals and accommodations). The following section describes various strategies and adaptations for Andrew, a high school student, during a social studies unit on map reading.

Table 4.2. Instructional support plan

Student	IEP	Same	ML	CO	Goals	Accommodations
Keisha	X	X			Meet general education curriculum goals.	Give extended time on tests.
Carlos	X			X	Use communication device to respond to peers.	Mount a variety of switches in the classroom(s) and leave them in place.
					Use switch to activate electronics.	Teach peers to program switches.
					Make choices when presented with three options.	Use daily schedule.
Andrew	X		X		Demonstrate five new concepts per unit.	Use written positive behavior support plan.

Key: IEP = individualized education program; ML = multilevel curriculum; CO = curriculum overlapping.

Andrew's Support Strategies and Adaptations

Andrew is a bright, personable freshman who attends his local high school. He is an avid sports fan; he likes to play basketball and the drums and enjoys surfing on the Internet. He is a curious learner, enjoys being with his classmates, and reads at the elementary level. His comprehension is significantly improved with the use of pictures. Andrew also has Down syndrome. Many of Andrew's IEP goals are written from a multilevel perspective. The following goals will be addressed during a unit on map reading in Andrew's social studies class:

1. *Acquire five new vocabulary terms per unit.*

2. *Use pictures to supplement written text in order to improve comprehension.*

During this unit, Andrew will

1. *Use local maps to navigate from his home or school to local areas of need or interest (see a photograph example of Andrew using local maps on this page).*

2. *Use a map to lay out the route for a family vacation.*

3. *Use an online map and direction aid to find directions between two locations.*

During this unit, Andrew will require the following adaptations:

1. *A multilevel curriculum*

2. *Two-column note taking*

3. *Pictures to align with his visual learning style in order to access the content of the instruction*

4. *The use of an online map and direction aid to sketch a map of his local community instead of doing it by hand*

The following instructional strategies will be used to support Andrew during this unit:

1. *A two-column note-taking strategy that combines pictures and words with text written at the second- to third-grade reading level*

2. *An online flashcard program*

Figure 4.3 shows an example of a two-column note-taking strategy for Andrew. Using Microsoft Word's Flesch–Kincaid reading level function, the set of notes in Figure 4.3 is calculated to be at the 2.2 grade level.

Curriculum Overlapping

Giangreco et al. defined curriculum overlapping as

> Teaching a diverse group of students within a shared activity in which students have different, individually appropriate learning outcomes that come from two or more curriculum areas (e.g., a student is pursuing communication learning outcomes in a science activity while other students have science learning outcomes). (1998, p. 12)

Types of maps	What they show
Road maps	Road maps show how people can travel from one place to another.
World maps	World maps show all of the continents and bodies of water.
Map reading	
Compass	Compasses show the directions of north, south, east, and west.
Latitude lines	Latitude lines go east and west.
Longitude lines	Longitude lines go north and south.

Figure 4.3. Example of two-column note taking for Andrew.

As with multilevel curriculum and instruction, some key components must be in place for curriculum overlapping to occur:

1. A "diverse group of students" refers to the classroom composition reflecting the natural diversity within the community. This includes all aspects of diversity (e.g., race, ability, socioeconomic status).

- *Practical application:* A classroom would include no more than 12% students with disabilities and 1% or fewer students with severe disabilities. The classroom would not be composed of 50% of students with disabilities or 100% of students with a particular type of disability (Vaughn, Bos, & Schumm, 2003).

2. "Shared activity" refers to all students participating in the same activity.

   - *Practical application:* All students, including the student(s) with disabilities, are participating in literacy centers.

3. "Different, individually appropriate learning outcomes within the context of the activity" indicates that some students' outcomes will differ from others'.

   - *Practical application:* A student with severe disabilities is working on switch activation in the listening center. Given a prompt from a peer, the student activates a switch that turns on the tape recorder and allows all members of the group to listen to a book on tape or use a program on the computer.

4. When two or more curriculum areas are involved, curriculum overlapping differs from multilevel curriculum and instruction. Typically, the curriculum areas that overlap come from the following academic areas or areas related to them: communication, socialization, health and safety, and daily life skills.

   - *Practical application:* During physics lab, Tomas, a high school student with severe intellectual disabilities (i.e., part of a diverse group of students), is engaged in a physics experiment on the topic of circuits (i.e., engaging in a shared activity). His learning outcomes are related to 1) following two-step directions (i.e., one curricular area); 2) initiating conversation with a same-age peer (i.e., a second curricular area for Tomas); and 3) making a transition between class activities (i.e., a third curricular area for Tomas). Physics lab provides a rich and interesting context for learning these important skills in relationship to his same-age peers. This shared environment also increases the likelihood that Tomas will engage in positive interdependence and build friendships.

WHAT ARE LEARNING OUTCOMES AND GENERAL SUPPORTS?

Students with and without disabilities attend school to learn a variety of academic, social, and communication skills. Teachers design instruction that increases the likelihood that students will attain targeted learning outcomes. *Learning outcomes* are those attitudes, skills, and abilities that students exhibit as a result of the instruction they have received. Learning outcomes result in a change in student behavior. All students should be working toward several learning outcomes simultaneously. Learning outcomes can be part of the general education curriculum via multilevel curriculum, such as reciting the multiplication tables, learning a foreign language, or reading at different levels. Learning outcomes can also be individual via curriculum overlapping, such as making choices between two activities, using a switch to activate a communication device, or managing a personal schedule. Whether the learning outcomes are related to the general education curriculum or are individual, they always focus on what the student is learning, and they involve the student in doing something new as a result of having engaged in instruction.

General supports refer to those things that adults or peers must do to or for the student with disabilities for the student to gain access to the learning environment (Giangreco et al., 1998). General supports do not require teaching on the part of adults or peers or learning on the part of the student. General supports include positioning a student so that he or she can see the board, putting splints on for a student, offering materials to a student in his or her first language, or providing enlarged print materials. Each of these responsibilities involves effort and management by someone other than the student. The student is not expected to acquire skills as a result of these efforts. Over time, general supports can evolve into learning outcomes, although they may not necessarily do so. For example, during the present school year, Mariah is not being taught how to manage her personal schedule. Instead, an adult is arranging the schedule. This task requires no learning on Mariah's part and therefore is a general support. However, next year the team may decide that it is appropriate to teach Mariah how to manage her own schedule. Managing a personal schedule would then become a learning outcome for her because the adults would design the instruction with the intention that Mariah learn to arrange her own daily schedule. As a learning outcome, managing a personal schedule would require effort and behavior change on Mariah's part.

ACTIVITY 8

Categorizing Goals and Objectives

As a team, look at a student's IEP. Read the goals and objectives aloud. Categorize the student's goals and objectives as

- Multilevel curriculum or curriculum overlapping
- Learning outcomes or general supports

What Did You Notice?

If a student's IEP is filled with general supports and has very few or no learning outcomes, the team has probably focused on what the teacher is doing instead of what the student should be learning as a result of instruction. Teaching and learning are, after all, inextricably linked. In such situations, your team should reexamine the IEP process and include learning outcomes for the student. Be certain that the student's family is involved in this process. Another thing you may discover is that the IEP has several goals that focus on decreasing or eliminating behaviors without specifying replacement behaviors. This approach leaves the team with little information about what to teach the student to do rather than to not do. However, if the student had a set of behaviors that were more meaningful and more powerful, he or she would use them to communicate needs or wants. Chapter 5 of this text will address this topic in more detail.

HOW DO WE ORGANIZE CURRICULUM PRIORITIES THROUGH DELIBERATE COMMUNICATION?

A simple organizational system can help teams track students' instructional needs in each class. The accommodations matrix shown in Table 4.3 is one example. This matrix gives an overview of students' needs to be incorporated during lesson planning. In the far right column, the teacher can make a note of which adaptations or accommodations can be generalized to the other students in the class. Most of the adaptations required by individual students actually benefit many students in the classroom. For example, a student with autism may require a personalized picture schedule, but most students would also benefit from the use of some type of daily schedule or planner. The teacher could post the daily schedule in the room and teach students to refer to it throughout the day. Although this is necessary for the student with autism, it is a practical aid for students of all ages and abilities as teachers support them in becoming responsible and independent.

 # Paraprofessional Self-Advocacy

Given the complexity of the information presented thus far in this chapter, now is a good time to check for understanding. Ask your team members to describe multilevel curriculum and curriculum overlapping in relationship to the students in the classrooms where you are or will be working.

Table 4.3. Accommodations matrix

Accommodations	Suki	Jevon	Rosa	Sam	Accommodations that may be helpful to the whole class
Seating	X				
Two-column note taking		X	X		X
Graphic organizers				X	X
Personal schedule	X	X	X	X	X
Individual to-do list				X	X

HOW CAN WE ARRANGE THE CLASSROOM ROUTINE TO SUPPORT DIVERSE LEARNERS?

When teachers have the opportunity to include students with disabilities as members of their classroom communities, often the traditional ways of doing things change. Although some of these changes are due to the unique needs of individual students, these changes or adaptations often benefit other students as well. For example, the teacher may implement an online flashcard program in a foreign language class to support a student with moderate disabilities in learning five basic words. The same program would be very helpful for the students who are preparing for the advanced placement exam. Accommodations that are helpful for many students include text-to-speech software, highlighting technology, graphic organizers, concept mapping software, to-do lists, personal planners, and various forms of PowerPoint. Each of these offers many students the opportunity to engage more independently in classroom events. Each reflects the functional skills that students need beyond the school doors.

The same can be true of specific instructional techniques. For example, a student's IEP might specify the use of delayed responding techniques during whole-class instruction. This instructional strategy can be used with all students in the class. Other specialized instructional techniques that may be helpful include prompting strategies, errorless learning when acquiring new concepts, and vocabulary strategies. These specialized instructional strategies are part of the special education teacher's repertoire and are worth sharing as a team. The special educator might teach one strategy per month to all members of the team. Included in the instruction should be the following:

1. Name and description of the strategy

2. Identification of the types of learners who would benefit from the strategy

3. Demonstration of the strategy in the general education classroom

4. Discussion of the implications of using the strategy

Another important consideration when arranging classroom routines to support unique learners is an intentional focus on teaching students to advocate for themselves. At the middle and high school levels, for example, Para Form 11: Student Learning Priorities and Support (see Chapter 3 for a filled-in version of this form; a blank version of this form is located in the Para Forms appendix), can give classroom teachers a good understanding of how the student with disabilities will participate in daily activities within the classroom. Clearly, this form has generalization potential. For example, team members can conduct a classroom meeting in which they describe the importance of students taking personal responsibility for their education. One way for all students to make some deliberate decisions about how they will participate in instruction is for them to check the items that are most appropriate for them on the Student Learning Priorities and Support worksheet. Generally, students make very appropriate decisions. If individual students make decisions you do not agree with, hold an individual conference with students with the intent of understanding their perspective. These are opportunities to find out what is really happening in a particular student's life.

Reflection

Examine your students' IEPs and instructional matrices. Identify the accommodations and instructional techniques individual students require. Then answer the following questions.

- In what ways might these same accommodations or instructional strategies benefit all students in the classroom?

- How will we rearrange what we currently do to incorporate these strategies into the daily routine?

HOW DOES UNIT PLANNING SUPPORT DIVERSE LEARNERS?

When planning an instructional unit, classroom teachers should assume that students have different levels of background knowledge about the topic. Students will also have different reading levels. Therefore, during planning, the general education teacher and special education teacher should develop text sets that represent different reading levels but are appropriate for students' chronological ages. For example, Mrs. Grant is preparing a unit on China for eighth-grade students. She has worked with the school librarian to gather materials that reflect sixth- through 10th-grade reading levels. However, Mrs. Grant has several students who read at the second- through fourth-grade levels. What should she do? First, Mrs. Grant should expand her search to include picture books, travel brochures, and selected web sites. Next, she should work with the special education teacher to identify high-interest, low-readability texts. In this case, the special education teacher searched materials from Wieser Educational and found a series titled *Tales of China: Retold Timeless Classics.* The books contain seven traditional Chinese stories written at the fourth-grade reading level. This prompted the general educator to design several of the reading comprehension lessons based on Chinese tales, using texts from different reading levels.

Another rather generic way to plan for participation by a student with disabilities is to identify the content the student will learn at the beginning of an instructional unit, not as an afterthought. If, for example, a student has a goal of learning three new concepts per unit of instruction and six related vocabulary terms, the classroom teacher should decide which concepts and vocabulary are key and communicate these to other team members (e.g., the paraprofessional, speech-language pathologist, special educator). The speech-language pathologist may take the lead in having the student work with the vocabulary terms (e.g., through articulation, comprehension, making connections, entering them into the flashcard program). The special educator would individualize instruction for the student, and the paraprofessional might preteach the vocabulary using the online flashcard program during study hall. Table 4.4 shows a simple way to track that content adapted for a student with disabilities over the duration of the instructional unit. Like all students, the student with disabilities will actively participate in all of the related learning activities of the unit, with a specific emphasis on the identified learning outcomes.

Table 4.4. Unit content adapted for a student with disabilities

Unit: Solar system Date: October	Adapted information: multilevel curriculum and instruction	Adapted information: curriculum overlapping
Concept 1: The organization of the solar system	There are nine planets.	Respond to two-step directions.
Concept 2: Two characteristics of earth	The earth is made up of land and water.	Use picture to-do list to complete tasks.
Concept 3: Rotation of the earth and sun	The earth revolves around the sun.	Use electric wheelchair to navigate around room and school.

Reflection

Think about the educational programs of the students with disabilities who are on your team. How would you describe these students' daily learning experiences? Are they engaged with their peers in rich and interesting units of instruction, or are they developing skills and filling out worksheets? Often, the more significant the disability, the more the program is based on skill. If this is true in your situation, I encourage you to change this practice quickly to reflect a more complex, interesting curriculum.

WHAT IS PRETEACHING?

The prefix "pre" means before, so *preteaching* simply refers to the teaching that happens before the main instruction begins. Preteaching aspects of a lesson (e.g., key vocabulary, two or three major concepts) can enable a student with moderate or severe disabilities to actively participate in the body of the lesson within a multilevel framework. In a middle or high school science class, for example, the students may be studying the process of photosynthesis. Most of the students have prior knowledge about the topic from previous classes. Grace, a student with severe disabilities, has very limited experience with related content knowledge and vocabulary; therefore, during her study hall class and speech therapy sessions she will work with a paraprofessional and the speech-language pathologist in preteaching situations. The focus of the preteaching will be 1) learning five related vocabulary terms using flashcards that combine words and images and 2) rehearsing placing a set of vocabulary cards on the teacher's desk when Grace walks into the room. The teacher will use the cards during whole-class instruction. For example, the teacher may ask Grace to find the flashcard with the picture of the plant while simultaneously holding up the correct response. This would combine picture prompts with errorless learning. Or the teacher may use an index card to prompt him- or herself as to which terms Grace has been studying, while overlaying the use of the delayed responding technique. For example, the teacher sees the index card, gives it back to Grace and says, "Grace, look at this picture for a few minutes and be ready to tell me the name of the plant. I will be back to you in a minute." Then the teacher moves on to another student before getting back to Grace. This offers Grace the delayed time to generate a response, without interfering with the flow of instruction.

In both scenarios, Grace has been taught content-related aspects of the lesson as well as a process-related element—specifically, placing the cards on the teacher's desk before she goes to her seat. This preteaching approach increases the likelihood that she will be an active participant with the content. With access to the information Grace has been learning, the teacher is more likely to deliberately include Grace in the course content.

Preteaching can involve traditional instructional content, behavioral rehearsal, and routine rehearsal. Any demand that is required in an inclusive setting can be rehearsed in advance. However, it is important for the team to remember that it is still the responsibility of the special educator or the general educator to design the instruction. For example, the teachers should indicate to the paraprofessional who is preteaching Grace whether to use a match-to-sample strategy, delayed responding techniques, system of least prompts, or system of most prompts. They also should explain what data will be collected and how frequently. Given the learning and performance characteristics of students with moderate and severe disabilities, it is important to have instructional consistency.

The timing of preteaching relative to involvement in general education classes must be individualized. In elementary school, preteaching may occur two or three times per day when students are engaged in individual instruction, giving the teacher, paraprofessional, or related services personnel an opportunity to preteach content within the inclusive classroom. At the middle and high school levels, it may mean scheduling a study hall in the morning and another in the afternoon before the general education classes. Keep in mind that, generally, there is no need to go to a resource room for this activity, especially at the high school level. Rather, preteaching should occur where students without disabilities go to study (e.g., cafeteria, library, specific room).

WHAT ARE THE COMMON COMPONENTS OF DAILY ROUTINES?

The previous sections have described the more generic approaches to the teaching and learning process for students with disabilities. Consider now some of the students with severe disabilities who require very specific instructional approaches to learn certain types of information. This specialized instruction is what special education is all about. One instructional approach is referred to as common sequential components of daily routines (Brown, Evans, Weed, & Owen, 1987). After the special educator has designed instruction for a student with disabilities and trained the paraprofessional in how to use this approach during a specific lesson, the paraprofessional can implement the instruction as designed.

People do many routine things on a daily basis. To learn what might be important to teach students with disabilities, Fredda Brown and colleagues (1987) studied how people in general go through their daily routines. They discovered that people go through all routines (e.g., getting up in the morning, opening mail at work, eating) in a similar sequence:

1. The routine has to be started or initiated.

2. The person has to prepare for the routine.

3.   The main part, or the core, of the activity or routine has to be done.

4.   The person has to end, or terminate, the activity or routine.

These four phases are referred to as common sequential components of daily routines (Brown et al., 1987, p. 119).

Common and sequential components are just that—common to all routines and carried out in a particular sequence. Here is a practical application of these four sequential components for getting to class on time and independently, an activity that is part of many elementary, middle, and high school routines:

1.   *Initiate:* Respond to bell by going to locker.

2.   *Prepare:* Open locker. Look at self in mirror. Read picture schedule taped to inside of door. Gather materials for next class and cross off on picture schedule.

3.   *Core:* Walk to class with peers. Take out homework. Place homework on edge of desk to be collected.

4.   *Terminate:* Wait for teacher directions.

These same four components apply to meeting personal care needs, such as utilizing assistance during lunch or in the bathroom. For example, a student who requires assistance with eating might have the following components:

1.   *Initiate:* Respond to personal schedule, indicating lunch as the next activity.

2.   *Prepare:* Gather and carry lunch items (e.g., lunchbox, tray).

3.   *Core:* Indicate "more" in response to the question "Do you want some more pretzels?" Hand is guided to the bowl of pretzels by a peer.

4.   *Terminate:* Go with peers to dispose of lunch trash.

All too often, adults intervene in a sequence by doing every step for the student except the core step. Although this might be more efficient in some situations, the student loses the opportunity to engage in the rhythm of the whole sequence, in which one step is a reminder for the next. The rhythm is vital to functional engagement in the routine. Even if the student can only partially participate during each phase, he or she should be supported to do that.

In addition to the four common sequential components of daily routines, Brown and colleagues (1987) identified five other components that are woven throughout many daily activities: communication, interaction with others, choice making, problem solving, and keeping track of time. Rainforth and York-Barr (1997) added movement and positioning to this list. This component emphasizes the essential role of movement between locations and the importance of effective positioning and movement of the body in all aspects of daily life. The interwoven components of routines are often not technically necessary for the completion of a routine. For example, a student can eat a meal by learning to chew and swallow;

however, if the student is taught how to communicate with others during a meal, the quality of that experience is improved. In addition, if the student communicates that he or she does not want certain foods, choice and control are increased. Interwoven components can occur at various times throughout a routine or an activity—they should not occur separately. For example, during the morning calendar routine, a student may need to walk up to the calendar (i.e., movement) and stand in front of the calendar (i.e., positioning) or talk with another student (i.e., communication and interaction). Because these interwoven components are part of the routine, it is very important that teams teach them as embedded skills within typical routines rather than as isolated components or skills out of context.

Becoming familiar with the common components framework can help your team consider the many learning opportunities available in general education classrooms as well as the types of supports that may be necessary for a student to gain access to those outcomes. The framework can also be used as a practical means of helping paraprofessionals provide only the necessary supports for students with and without disabilities.

Here is an example of how the common components framework might be used to help a student learn a routine. Upon completing a picture schedule sample for the student as seen in Figure 4.4, the special educator clearly communicates to the teacher and paraprofessional that the student is responsible for gathering his or her own materials for class (e.g., appropriate textbook, pencil, folder). The student will be taught to do this by using his or her personalized picture or object schedule that lists the items needed for each class. The paraprofessional will tap the student's schedule 5 minutes before the end of class to prompt the student to 1) put away materials from the current class and 2) take out the materials for the next class. The goal is that after 2 weeks of prompting, the paraprofessional will no longer cue the student, and the student will check off the materials. These steps are part of the student's instructional priorities. The cueing is part of the instructional intervention.

As a team, you can use this framework to consistently approach and teach active participation in the many routines that are a part of every school day. It is critical that the team plan into the instruction ways for various people (e.g., peers, teachers, classroom volunteers) to support the student's learning. To become more familiar with the framework's application to instruction, refer to the following forms (a filled-out version of each para form appears in this chapter as Figures 4.5, 4.6, and 4.7; blank versions of these forms are located in the Para Forms appendix):

- Para Form 13: Common Components of Daily Routines: Practice with a Familiar Routine

- Para Form 14: Common Components of Daily Routines: Apply to a Student's Schedule

- Para Form 15: Common Components of Daily Routines: Planning Worksheet

Use the first para form to apply the framework to a daily routine that is familiar to you. By applying this strategy to your own circumstances, it may be easier to generalize it to students' circumstances. The remaining two worksheets can be used for applying the common components framework to a student's routine in school.

Figure 4.4. Sample picture schedule. (Picture Communication Symbols © 1981–2007 by Mayer-Johnson LLC. All rights reserved worldwide. Used with permission; Boardmaker™ is a trademark of Mayer-Johnson LLC.)

Four Sequential Components of Daily Routines

For many students with disabilities, the four sequential components of daily routines are important to consider when determining learning priorities and designing individualized instruction programs. Think about a daily routine in which the paraprofessional supports a student:

- Does the paraprofessional focus primarily on the core elements of the instructional sequence, or does he or she facilitate the student's progress through all four phases?

- What is the student's cue or prompt to get started?

- When cued or prompted, does the student prepare for the routine?

Common Components of Daily Routines
Apply to a Student's Schedule

Directions: As a team, apply the common components framework to an activity or routine that a student engages in daily. First, consider how the student does or could participate in each component. Then, consider how to support the student in participating in each component.

Student: _Jack Parkhurst_

Routine or activity: _Solving double-digit problems with a calculator_

	Student participation What will the student do? Where will the student be?	Support What will you do? Where will you be?
Initiate How do you know it's time to begin this activity (e.g., alarm rings, refer to your personal schedule)?	• Bell rings • Look at picture schedule	• Para in classroom • Not in close proximity to Jack
Prepare What do you need to do in order to be ready for the activity (e.g., gather certain materials)?	• Gather math book, notebook, pencil and calculator	• If Jack doesn't respond and a classmate doesn't help, para moves in to provide support
Core What do you actually do? How do you participate?	• Match sample number on calculator with number on worksheet.	• Gestural prompts • Model
Terminate How do you know when the activity is over?	• Teacher stops lesson • Pack up materials	• Same as initiate
As part of this routine, which interwoven components will be targeted for instruction or support (e.g., communication, interaction with others, choice making, problem solving)?		

From Brown, F., Evans, I., Weed, K., & Owen, V. (1987). Delineating functional competencies: A component model. *Journal of The Association for Persons with Severe Handicaps, 12*(2), 199; adapted by permission.

In *The Paraprofessional's Guide to the Inclusive Classroom: Working as a Team* by Mary Beth Doyle (2008).

Figure 4.6. Example of Para Form 14: Common Components of Daily Routines: Apply to a Student's Schedule.

Common Components of Daily Routines
Practice with a Familiar Routine

Directions: Apply the common components framework to a typical activity or routine that you engage in every day.

Student: _Sarah_

Routine or activity: _Transitions between classes_

	Your participation
Initiate How do you know it is time to begin this activity (e.g., alarm rings, refer to your personal schedule)?	1. Teacher: "Pack up your things."
Prepare What do you need to do in order to be ready for the activity (e.g., gather certain materials)?	2. Put my things in my backpack. 3. Bell rings.
Core What do you actually do? How do you participate?	4. Nod to classmate indicating he can push my wheelchair.
Terminate How do you know when the activity is over?	5. Go to next class together chatting along the way. 6. Take out things.
As part of this routine, which interwoven components will be targeted for instruction or support (e.g., communication, interaction with others, choice making, problem solving)?	

From Brown, F., Evans, I., Weed, K., & Owen, V. (1987). Delineating functional competencies: A component model. *Journal of the Association for Persons with Severe Handicaps, 12*(2), 199 adapted by permission.

In *The Paraprofessional's Guide to the Inclusive Classroom: Working as a Team* by Mary Beth Doyle (2008).

Figure 4.5. Example of Para Form 13: Common Components of Daily Routines: Practice with a Familiar Routine.

- Are there necessary materials that must be gathered?
- What is the core of the activity or routine?
- Is the paraprofessional teaching the student to bring closure to the activity or routine?
- Do all members of the team approach the routines in a similar way, thereby increasing instructional consistency?

Paraprofessional Self-Advocacy

Try to envision the common components of a variety of typical daily routines and activities. Ask the special educator about expectations related to common components of daily routines.

■■■ PARA FORM 15 ■■■

Common Components of Daily Routines
Planning Worksheet

Directions: Use this form with Para Form 14: Common Components of Daily Routines: Apply to a Student's Schedule to describe which interwoven components will be targeted for each major daily routine.

Student: _Keisha Martin_

Routine or activity: _Making independent transitions_

	Student participation What will the student do? Where will the student be?	Support What will you do? Where will you be?
Communication		
Interacting with others	Talk with Jill and Paul while changing classes	No adults necessary
Choice making		
Problem solving		
Monitoring quality		
Monitoring tempo	Must arrive at each class on time	Check attendance records for tardiness and mark if on time or late
Movement and positioning		

Figure 4.7. Example of Para Form 15: Common Components of Daily Routines: Planning Worksheet.

WHAT IS PARTIAL PARTICIPATION?

Independence is not always the desired outcome when people with or without disabilities engage in a variety of daily activities. In reality, much of adults' lives are spent living in interdependent relationships and activities. Often, people live with someone they choose, prepare and eat meals together, help each other with daily chores, and carpool to work, for example. One person may do the grocery shopping and the other may balance the checkbook. One may wash the laundry and the other put the laundry away. Similarly, children often participate partially in a wide variety of activities or responsibilities before they are able to complete an entire activity. A young child might pour cereal into a bowl; an older sibling might pour in the milk. An adolescent might weed the garden and the parent might mow the lawn. Both children and adults partially participate in a wide variety of activities before they master them.

As early as 1982, Diane Baumgart and her colleagues applied this concept to supporting students with severe disabilities in actively participating in inclusive classrooms. Partial participation affirms that students with severe disabilities can be supported in participating, at least in part, in a variety of age-appropriate activities in school, home, and community environments (Ferguson & Baumgart, 1991).

There are several things to keep in mind as your team uses this concept. First, it is critical that each team member understand and support the concept of partial participation, because attitudes do shape how support is delivered. Those who espouse partial participation as a legitimate option for engaging in learning activities are more likely to say, "Of course we can figure out how John can participate in this activity."

Second, although the expectation for the student with disabilities may not be independent mastery, there are still specific instructional goals (as part of multilevel curriculum or curriculum overlapping) for the student within the context of the activity. For example, during a science lab, a student with severe disabilities may be participating in part (e.g., learning one new vocabulary term), tracking the steps of the lab using a picture list of stages, and responding to interactions of peers, all within the context of the instruction. Therefore, the team needs to be clear about the student's IEP goals and the appropriate instructional strategies, supports, and adaptations or accommodations required. If a paraprofessional is providing support during the lesson, he or she will need this information, too.

When combining the concept of partial participation with common components of daily routines and curriculum overlapping, the instructional opportunities are endless. In combination, they complement one another and allow students with a wide range of characteristics and abilities to participate in almost every class activity. The implicit messages that teachers send when every student is welcomed, supported, and included in the typical course of daily routines are powerful. There can be a subtle shift in attitude from a focus on what students cannot do to what aspects of an activity they can and will learn to do. As teachers model the expectations of active engagement and participation, so too will students. A pervasive attitude of partial participation is the cornerstone of all inclusive classrooms.

HOW ARE INSTRUCTIONAL PROMPTS PROVIDED?

Everyone responds to cues in their daily lives. Cues are prompts that help people remember when or how to do certain things. For example, to wake up in the morning, some people are cued or prompted by sunlight streaming in, others are prompted by an alarm clock, and still others need to be shaken vigorously. You may have noticed that some of these cues are stronger or more intense than others. As presented, the cues move from the least intrusive or most natural (e.g., the rising sun) to the most intrusive or most unnatural (e.g., the involvement of another person).

At school, students also respond to cues throughout the day. For example, a bell rings as a cue to change classes, a teacher enters the classroom as a cue for students to return to their desks, or a teacher says, "Turn to page 62" as a cue to turn to the appropriate page in the textbook. Often, students are not taught directly to respond to certain cues, but they learn through observation, by trial and error, or with help from a friend. However, some students need to be taught directly how to respond to specific cues in order to participate in daily activities at school. These students require carefully designed cueing or prompting strategies. Determining the type and intensity of a cue to facilitate student participation requires consideration of the student's unique learning characteristics and of the specific activity and its context.

When learning a new skill, some students need a prompt (e.g., pointing, a nudge, a hint) added to the naturally occurring cue to respond when participating in an activity or routine. Usually, a prompt is added only after the student fails to respond to the natural cue. Some students may need physical help in the form of hand-over-hand assistance from a peer, and others may simply need a visual reminder. For example, when it is time to change classes, the bell rings. Most students stand up, gather their belongings, move toward the door, and exit. If a student fails to respond to the natural cues of the bell ringing and the students walking out, he or she may need to be told, "When you hear the bell ring and see the other kids stand up, get your things, check your schedule, and go to your next class." This verbal prompt may be accompanied by a gesture (e.g., pointing to classmates leaving).

The type and level of prompt should be individualized for each student and for each activity, typically by the special educator. It is not unusual for a student to require a different type or amount of assistance in different activities. Do not assume that if a student requires hand-over-hand assistance for one activity, he or she will require it for another. The type and amount of support is specifically intended to result in the student eventually learning to be as independent (or, in some cases, as interdependent) as possible. Making cues and prompts more consistent can increase the rate at which students learn specific tasks and routines.

Table 4.5 lists seven common types of instructional prompts that are ordered from the least intrusive to the most intrusive. This is not meant to suggest that prompts should always

Table 4.5. Instructional prompts

Prompt	Definition	Example
Natural	An ordinary cue to get started; naturally exists in the environment	The bell rings for class.
Gestural	Physical movement to communicate or accentuate a cue (e.g., arm and hand movement, head nod)	The teacher points to the chalkboard.
Indirect verbal	Verbal statement or reminder that prompts the student to attend to another cue or to think about and recognize what is expected	"I'm glad to see that so many children are in a straight line."
Direct verbal	Specific verbal direction	"Joe, please get in line."
Modeling	Demonstration of what the student is supposed to do	A student demonstrates how to write the letter *A*. Another student copies that example.
Partial physical	Physical assistance for a portion of the activity or a part of the total movement required for the activity	One student places a pen in another student's hand. The receiving student grasps the pen.
Full physical	Physical assistance to complete an activity (e.g., hand-over-hand assistance)	The paraprofessional places and maintains his hands over the student's hands to reach, grasp, and manipulate the computer controls.

be provided in this order. For example, a student may be overdependent on verbal cues to initiate activities. In this situation, pointing or a nudge may actually be less intrusive than a verbal cue. This student may need to learn to use visual cues instead of auditory cues only.

Paraprofessional Self-Advocacy

If you have not received direction from the teachers as to the type of prompting strategy to use with a student, ask for what you need. For example, you might say, "During this type of small-group activity, what type(s) of instructional prompting does Marcus need? Who should provide it? Will you model it for me in the general education classroom?" This frank yet respectful questioning supports the whole team in considering students' specific instructional needs.

Para Form 16: Discussion of Prompting Strategies worksheet (see Figure 4.8 for a filled-out version in this chapter; a blank version of this form appears in the Para Forms appendix) offers a guide for team discussion and application of concepts related to instructional prompting. Prior to beginning this discussion, have your team list four of a student's learning priorities (from the student's IEP) in the left column of the worksheet. Then, as a team, discuss and check the prompt or prompts listed in the center column that are most likely to assist this student in accomplishing each learning priority. Finally, discuss and identify who (i.e., classmates or adults) might provide this assistance. It is important to guard against students' overreliance on adult assistance, specifically paraprofessional assistance. Such overreliance decreases the likelihood that students will help one another, and adults then become barriers to student interactions and participation.

After your discussion, team members should ask the special educator to demonstrate how to apply instructional prompts when working with the student. The demonstration should take place in the same locations and during the same activities that the prompting is required, as demonstration in context is more effective than demonstration out of context. This is because within the classroom, the special educator must attend to and incorporate all of the naturally occurring activities, just as the classroom teacher and paraprofessional will have to during actual instruction.

HOW ARE CURRICULAR ADAPTATIONS USED?

An adaptation is "any adjustment or modification in the curriculum, instruction, environment, or materials in order to enhance the participation of a member of the classroom community" (Udvari-Solner, 1992, p. 3). Many students with and without disabilities use adaptations to accomplish tasks more efficiently and to participate more fully in classroom activities. Common examples are homework assignment books, calculators, and computers. Adaptations should:

- Be appropriate for the student's chronological age and incorporate age-appropriate materials
- Promote active participation and interaction for the student with disabilities
- Build on the student's strengths
- Enhance the student's status and thereby promote positive self-esteem
- Avoid being intrusive

There are three general categories of adaptations:

- Adaptations that are constant over time
- Adaptations that are short term and preplanned
- Adaptations that need to be developed on the spot

Constant Over Time

The first type of adaptation is constant or unchanging over time; these adaptations are used frequently by the student in various situations throughout the day. They are developed or acquired at a specific moment in time and used over an extended period. Examples include computers, wheelchairs, communication systems, positioning equipment, individualized picture schedules, adaptive switches, large-size computer keyboards, and calculators. It is important for each member of the education team to become acquainted with these student-specific adaptations, how the student should use the adaptations, and the type of support (e.g., cues) required for the student to use them. Although the paraprofessional may be asked to assist in the development or acquisition of constant adaptations, it is typically the responsibility of a certified team member (e.g., general educator, special educator, related services personnel) to acquire or design them.

PARA FORM 16

Discussion of Prompting Strategies

Directions: The purpose of this worksheet is to guide your team in discussing a variety of instructional prompts. List four of the student's learning priorities (from the student's IEP) in the first column. Then, as a team, discuss and identify the type of prompts that are likely to assist this student in accomplishing each learning priority. Finally, discuss and identify the people who might provide this assistance.

Student: _Tony_

Learning priorities	Types of prompts	Who might provide this assistance?
Arrival • Greet friends • Locate partner for the day • Put items in locker • Gather necessary materials • Go to first class with peer	____ Natural _X_ Gestural ____ Indirect verbal _X_ Direct verbal ____ Model ____ Partial physical ____ Full physical	_X_ Classmates ____ Adults
Reading • Choose book, gather tape recorder and cassette tape • Use switch to activate taped stories • Put materials away	____ Natural _X_ Gestural _X_ Indirect verbal ____ Direct verbal ____ Model ____ Partial physical ____ Full physical	_X_ Classmates ____ Adults
Science • Participate in experiments (Note: Tony may need partial physical assistance. Be careful not to help him too much. Give him the opportunity to participate on his own. Classmates may provide assistance.)	____ Natural _X_ Gestural ____ Indirect verbal ____ Direct verbal ____ Model _X_ Partial physical ____ Full physical	_X_ Classmates _X_ Adults
Social Studies • Use online flashcard program to study vocabulary terms • Print teacher's PowerPoint slides	____ Natural _X_ Gestural ____ Indirect verbal _X_ Direct verbal ____ Model ____ Partial physical ____ Full physical	_X_ Classmates _X_ Adults

Figure 4.8. Example of Para Form 16: Discussion of Prompting Strategies.

Short Term and Preplanned

The second type of adaptation is short term and preplanned. These adaptations are usually specific to a given instructional unit or activity. Examples include using a modified worksheet that requires fewer responses or activating a prerecorded speech to participate in a school play. These adaptations are used for a shorter period of time than constant adaptations and are generally context specific. General and special educators are typically responsible for the design of short-term adaptations; however, paraprofessionals are often asked to assist in their development or refinement.

On the Spot

The third type of adaptation is developed on the spot in response to an activity that is about to occur or is in the process of occurring. For example, the general educator may decide to have the class paint a mural but may have no opportunity for prior discussion about how a student with multiple disabilities might participate. On the spot, classmates, the paraprofessional, or the general educator may be able to suggest several ways this student might participate. In another situation, the preplanned adaptation simply might not work, and a member of the classroom community (e.g., peer, volunteer) may need to quickly develop a new way for the student with disabilities to participate. In this case, the paraprofessional or other team member should do his or her best to generate an on-the-spot adaptation on the basis of the student's background and the specific activity. Classmates often provide excellent suggestions.

Streamlining Accommodations at the High School Level

Due to the number of students a high school teacher has, and the number of teachers each student has, teams at the high school level face particular communication challenges. This is especially true when students have moderate or severe disabilities. It is common for a high school teacher to have 80–125 students, each of whom has individual needs. A very important question emerges: In what ways can your team build systems of support around teachers to ensure that the needs of students with moderate or severe disabilities are met, particularly in regards to adaptations? Following are some answers:

- The special educator should give each team member an instruction matrix, such as the sample shown in Figure 4.9, that highlights goals, adaptations, and supports for the student(s) with disabilities.

- Team members can use the matrix as a data collection tool. For example, if the speech-language pathologist uses the vocabulary flashcards from science class, he or she would initial and date the appropriate box on the matrix. If the paraprofessional preteaches content during a structured study hall, he or she would initial the appropriate box. Over time, the special educator should study the matrix to identify instructional patterns and needs.

Instruction Matrix

Student: __Maria__   Subject: __Social Studies__   Unit topic: __Civil War__   Date: __October 1–November 1__

Directions: Place materials in binder for student and team to use.

	Read textbook pictures. Put Post-It notes on pictures.	Study **bold** words. Read. Write. Use in sentences.	Make flashcards of **bold** words.	Make flashcards online.	Make PowerPoint presentations with pictures.	Print PowerPoint presentations in two-column note-taking option.	Find five "school safe" related web sites and list in folder.
Textbook	☐ GE ☐ SE ☑ Para ☐ Peer:	☐ GE ☐ SE ☑ Para ☐ Peer:	☐ GE ☐ SE ☑ Para ☐ Peer:	☐ GE ☐ SE ☑ Para ☐ Peer:	☐ GE ☐ SE ☐ Para ☐ Peer:	☐ GE ☐ SE ☐ Para ☐ Peer:	☐ GE ☐ SE ☐ Para ☐ Peer:
Supplemental reading text or teacher-created text	☐ GE ☐ SE ☐ Para ☐ Peer:	☐ GE ☐ SE ☐ Para ☐ Peer:	☐ GE ☑ SE ☐ Para ☐ Peer:	☐ GE ☐ SE ☐ Para ☑ Peer:	☐ GE ☐ SE ☑ Para ☐ Peer:	☑ GE ☐ SE ☐ Para ☐ Peer:	☑ GE ☑ SE ☐ Para ☐ Peer:
Teacher-created notes	☐ GE ☐ SE ☐ Para ☐ Peer:	☐ GE ☐ SE ☐ Para ☐ Peer:	☐ GE ☐ SE ☐ Para ☐ Peer:	☐ GE ☐ SE ☐ Para ☐ Peer:	☑ GE ☐ SE ☐ Para ☐ Peer:	☐ GE ☐ SE ☐ Para ☐ Peer:	☐ GE ☐ SE ☐ Para ☐ Peer:
Teacher-created comprehension quiz	☐ GE ☐ SE ☐ Para ☐ Peer:	☐ GE ☐ SE ☐ Para ☐ Peer:	☐ GE ☐ SE ☐ Para ☐ Peer:	☐ GE ☐ SE ☐ Para ☐ Peer:	☐ GE ☑ SE ☐ Para ☐ Peer:	☑ GE ☐ SE ☐ Para ☐ Peer:	☐ GE ☐ SE ☐ Para ☐ Peer:

Team 1. Above reflects activities that need to be accomplished for every unit.
2. Please √ completion of each activity. Write notes on the back of this page if necessary.
3. There will not always be a supplemental text. In these cases please emphasize pictures, reading, and vocabulary from text.

Figure 4.9. Instruction matrix. (*Key:* GE = general educator, SE = special educator, Para = paraprofessional.)

- Each team should discuss which adaptations and accommodations that are required by some students would be helpful to most students.

- Each special education teacher can look at the IEPs of his or her students and list all of the identified accommodations, then answer these questions: Are there similarities across the accommodations? In what ways might I make the accommodations more similar, thereby decreasing the numbers of accommodations that the general education teachers need to remember? For example, one student requires a copy of the teacher's notes, another requires two-column note taking, and a third requires pictures. One adaptation that would meet the needs of all three students *and* be helpful for the rest of the class would be the use of PowerPoint slides as a note-taking system. This would require that the students be taught how to print a version of the presentation in a format that works for each of them. This could be taught at school during study hall or at home. Although the goal is certainly not to develop one solution for all students, teachers will be better equipped to juggle students' individual needs if there is some consistency.

WHAT IS DELAYED RESPONDING?

Delayed responding is a relatively simple instructional technique that general education teachers can use to support the participation of students who have processing delays of any type. The teacher simply asks the student a question and ends it with the statement "I'll get back to you in a minute for that answer." The teacher continues the class discussion while the student locates the answer. During this time the student has the option (or can be supported by a peer) to

- Find the answer in the book or notebook

- Ask a peer for the answer

- State the answer

- Get it correct

- Get it wrong

Delayed responding can be useful for a variety of students with and without disabilities. Delayed responding can be effective in any context. For example, during math class Mr. Smith writes a problem on the board and says to Thomas, a student with disabilities, "Thomas, I want you to calculate the solution to this problem, and I'll be back to you in a minute." Mr. Smith continues with the lesson while Thomas completes the problem. Returning to Thomas, Mr. Smith says, "Okay, Thomas, you were working on the solution to this problem. What did you figure out?" After the response is given, Mr. Smith makes the connection to the lesson at hand and continues with instruction. Delayed responding strategy has been used in classrooms for many years. The deliberate use of this strategy with students with disabilities is simply a new application of it.

HOW CAN NOTE-TAKING STRATEGIES
SUPPORT A VARIETY OF STUDENTS?

During middle and high school, students form an increasing number of relationships with a variety of adults. Typically, students move from having one classroom teacher (e.g., in elementary school) to having several content-area teachers (e.g., math, English, social studies). As the numbers of adult interactions increase, so too does the complexity of communication between teachers and families, and this happens at a time when communication is critical. If parents of middle and high school students are aware of the content being taught in the classroom, they are better able to provide supplemental supports at home (e.g., discussions at dinner, assistance with homework).

There are a variety of strategies for taking class notes, including audio-taping classes, having a peer use no carbon required (NCR) paper to take notes, using online flashcard programs, or getting notes from the teacher in either a two-column format or graphic organizing format. The latter can be shared with any student who would like them. The purpose of note taking is to support students in remembering key instructional facts.

If a paraprofessional is assigned to the class, it might be appropriate for the paraprofessional and classroom teacher to set up an adapted note-taking system, in which the paraprofessional uses a specific note-taking strategy to take notes and places the notes in a classroom binder for any student, including the student with disabilities, to access. This is an example of how a necessary accommodation for the student with disabilities can benefit the whole class.

The classroom teacher or special educator should indicate which specific note-taking strategy the paraprofessional should use with students. For example, visual notes (e.g., two-column note taking, graphic organizers) will be helpful for some students. The types of visuals are determined by the team. For example, pictures with short descriptions will be helpful for some students, whereas other students will need more formal picture symbols.

The two-column note-taking strategy involves dividing a sheet of notebook paper into two columns and writing the main points in the left column and supporting details in the right column. Pictures or icons may also be added.

Whenever an individual student requires specific support in classes, teams are encouraged to pose the question "In what ways might other classmates benefit from this same support?" In this situation, the answer is as simple: The paraprofessional can create and maintain a classroom notebook with daily notes that are made available to any student who has missed them for whatever reason.

PULLING IT ALL TOGETHER

Throughout this chapter, your team has been exposed to strategies for designing consistent approaches to curricular and instructional support for students. These strategies include

- Multilevel curriculum instruction and overlapping curriculum
- Learning outcomes and general supports

PARA FORM 17

Instructional Support Plan

Directions: Team members can use this form to document student learning priorities, appropriate prompts, and adaptations. For the last column, you can list both ongoing adaptations and preplanned, unit-specific adaptations.

Student: Lisa

General educator: Mr. Callao

Special educator: Ms. De la Rosa

Paraprofessional: Ms. Norman

Activity	Learning priorities	Instructional prompts		Suggested adaptations
1	For the whole class: double-digit addition For the student: double-digit addition	___ Natural X Gestural ___ Indirect verbal Y Direct verbal ___ Model ___ Partial physical ___ Full physical	X Peer X General educator ___ Special educator Y Paraprofessional ___ Related service personnel	Ongoing adaptation: Communication board Unit-specific accommodation: Calculator with large key pads
2	For the whole class: Identify the continents For the student: Locate North America	___ Natural X Gestural ___ Indirect verbal ___ Direct verbal ___ Model ___ Partial physical ___ Full physical	X Peer X General educator ___ Special educator ___ Paraprofessional ___ Related service personnel	Ongoing adaptation: Communication board Unit-specific accommodation: Match-to-sample cards Picture to accompany reading materials
3	For the whole class: For the student:	___ Natural ___ Gestural ___ Indirect verbal ___ Direct verbal ___ Model ___ Partial physical ___ Full physical	___ Peer ___ General educator ___ Special educator ___ Paraprofessional ___ Related service personnel	Ongoing adaptation: Unit-specific accommodation:

Figure 4.10. Example of Para Form 17: Instructional Support Plan.

- Common components of daily routines
- Partial participation
- Instructional prompts
- Curricular adaptations
- Note-taking strategies

Your team now has the opportunity to pull together the resources from this chapter into a more useable format. Para Form 17: Instructional Support Plan (see Figure 4.10 for the filled-out version in this chapter; a blank version of this form appears in the Para Forms appendix) is designed to assist your team with organizing the curriculum information for an individual student with disabilities and how he or she will participate in an instructional unit or a lesson plan. By using this worksheet regularly, your team will discover an increased sense of efficiency and a better use of staff time. I recommend that your team use the Instructional Support Plan as a planning tool prior to implementing new units of study in the general education curriculum (as opposed to daily lesson planning). This planning increases the likelihood that each team member will clearly understand the instructional focus for the student with disabilities. In addition, this planning ensures that paraprofessional's role and responsibilities are clear and well considered.

5

Encouraging Positive Behaviors

Objectives

- Apply the underlying tenets of PBS
- Discuss the five purposes of behaviors
- Discuss proactive strategies for supporting students in choosing to engage in appropriate behaviors
- Apply data collection strategies to interpreting challenging, disruptive, or unusual behaviors
- Design student-specific PBS plans

As you read about the role of paraprofessionals in supporting students who display challenging behaviors, it is important to remember that everyone engages in a variety of behaviors to communicate their needs, wants, and desires. Sometimes their behaviors align with their intentions; sometimes they do not. Often, people rely on others to interpret their behaviors and respond to them; when others respond in a way that does not align with their intentions, they simply clarify the intended meaning. For some students, behaviors are the primary ways in which they communicate, and many of these students do not have the ability to clarify their intentions through language (e.g., speech, sign language, picture communication). For example, on a hot day a student with severe disabilities begins to get upset and cries. The adult responds by giving the student a drink of water. The student continues to cry and the adult is perplexed as to why the student's behavior does not change. The short answer is that the adult's response did not match the student's communication intent. Perhaps the student wasn't thirsty, but hungry; perhaps the student wanted to go swimming or had a headache. Whatever the student's intention, the adult missed the mark. To minimize such misunderstandings, all members of the instructional team must have a deep understanding of the principles of PBS.

WHAT ARE THE FIVE TENETS OF POSITIVE BEHAVIORAL SUPPORT?

The following tenets, or underlying assumptions, can guide your thinking in many challenging situations and help you react in ways that are most constructive and supportive of students. It is important for teachers to guide, teach, and support paraprofessionals in coming to live by these underlying assumptions so that all members of the educational team will act consistently when a student displays unusual, disruptive, or challenging behavior. The underlying tenets of PBS are

1. All children and youth are inherently good.

2. Adults in the classroom significantly affect the quality of the atmosphere for all students.

3. All behavior is an attempt to communicate.

4. Power and control are not effective ways to shape students' behaviors.

5. Treat students as you would like to be treated.

All Children and Youth Are Inherently Good

Despite the way students might act or what they may say, each one has qualities and attributes that reflect goodness. Be careful not to overlook a particular student's good qualities. To support the learning and growth of all students, particularly those who display unusual, challenging, or disruptive behaviors, every team member must truly believe this tenet. In addition, you must all communicate this message consistently in an ongoing and unconditional manner to the students and to one another.

This first tenet is the foundation of PBS because adults' behaviors communicate subtle and not-so-subtle messages to students. When adults perceive students as challenging and do not genuinely and demonstratively care about them, they behave in ways that communicate this to students. These messages cause students to feel a sense of hurt, rejection, and failure to meet expectations. When students feel hurt and rejection, they react in ways that many people find challenging. In these situations the stage is set for a continuous, challenging cycle of disruptive behaviors. It is important to separate the student's behaviors from his or her inherent goodness and worth. One has nothing to do with the other. It is the responsibility of every adult member of the team to search for and bring out the inherent goodness of each student.

ACTIVITY 9

Positive Statements About Kids

Take a moment to write down the names of the students with whom you work and about whom you can quickly say, "What terrific kids!" What is it about these kids that you really enjoy? What is it about them that makes it easy to identify them as really *good kids*? Did other members of your team identify the same students? Clearly, you believe Tenet 1 in relationship to the students who came to your mind quickly.

Now think about the students who did not come to mind initially. What are their names? What do they look like and sound like? Who are their friends? Which adults care most about these students? Ask yourself why their goodness did not come to your mind immediately. Are they really so different from their peers? Keep thinking about those students. Do you find them particularly challenging? Search your experiences, and generate at least five positive statements about each of them. Do this every day until it becomes easy. If you find it a challenge to articulate the good qualities of any particular student, work with the other members of your team to generate these statements every day until they roll off your tongue like honey! It is impossible to truly teach someone if you do not believe in their inherent goodness because teaching begins with a relationship. If you do not have a relationship with a particular student, that student will feel little desire to learn from you.

Adults in the Classroom Significantly Affect the Quality of the Atmosphere for All Students

Adults have a significant impact on the quality of the atmosphere in the classroom. Teachers and paraprofessionals can make or break a student's day. A simple smile, a kind word, or a gentle touch go a long way in communicating the message "You are an important member of this community, and I am glad that you are here." Such kind gestures increase the likelihood that all students will feel welcomed and will respond in equally kind ways to other members of their community.

Some students do not react immediately to acts of kindness and welcome, or their reactions may be difficult to interpret. Some students make it difficult for adults to find ways to communicate kindness. However, this is exactly why teachers are entrusted with shaping the lives of children and youth: They have the professional skills and responsibility to continually deliver the core messages of unconditional welcome and support to all. Teachers can also support paraprofessionals in learning how to communicate messages of kindness and understanding. If a student does not feel a sense of welcome, connection, or belonging, it is very difficult for him or her to consider learning as a top priority in life. Expressing kindness and support for all students creates an atmosphere of acceptance and emotional safety.

ACTIVITY 10

Creating a Positive Atmosphere

Activity Form 10: Creating a Positive Atmosphere (located in the Activities appendix) highlights several ways in which adults in the classroom can create a positive atmosphere in which to carry out the important work of teaching children and youth. After reviewing the list, identify three or four additional things that your team does or would like to do to build a positive atmosphere. As a team, identify students who are on the fringes of the classroom community or who are often overlooked. Then discuss the following questions:

1. In what ways will I help this student feel a sense of welcome and belonging?

2. Specifically, what will I do and say?

3. How will I do these things when the student is in his or her most vulnerable state (e.g., acting out, not following instructions, being unkind to others)?

All Behavior Is an Attempt to Communicate

Often, the communicative intent of a student's behavior is fairly clear. For example, upon learning that he was not chosen to be in the school play, Bob kicks the ground and says, "I didn't really want to be in the play anyway…it's stupid." Clearly, the true communicative intent is disappointment, even though the student did not explicitly state that emotion. In essence, the student deflected the disappointment using another response. As time goes on and this student receives feedback from people in his life, he will become better able to handle the disappointments that are a part of everyone's life.

However, some students' reactions are more intense, last longer, or are out of proportion to the situation. In these situations, members of the educational team need to work together to better understand the communicative function of the behavior and to support students in finding more acceptable ways of communicating their needs to others. Some students need direct, consistent instruction in this area.

For students who have difficulty with traditional forms of communication (e.g., spoken language, sign language, written language), it can be harder to determine the communicative intent of their behaviors. Often, in an attempt to make themselves understood, they exhibit behaviors that are not acceptable in typical contexts (e.g., classroom, home, community). This increased intensity is fairly understandable. Imagine that you are unable to speak, write, or use sign language very effectively. Now imagine that you have a migraine headache. How would you tell someone? What if others could not understand that your migraine had been lingering for days? How could you communicate to them that every time they switch on a light or the radio or speak in a loud voice, your head hurts terribly? Might you pull at your head, tap it, or hit it? Perhaps you would cry endlessly or refuse to eat or to go to work. Unfortunately, if you were to engage in any of these behaviors, some people would say that you are being self-abusive. Given this interpretation, someone might attempt to restrain your hands. Others might say that you are being noncompliant or avoiding the task at hand, so they simply ignore you. The responses from each person are likely to be different based on his or her interpretation of the behavior. Unfortunately, as those around you are responding through three common behavior modification techniques—while a third person might reinforce you for being quiet (i.e., differential reinforcement of incompatible behaviors)—you are still left with an untreated migraine headache.

Now imagine that you can speak very clearly. You are a 15-year-old high school freshman who reads at the fifth-grade level. You are embarrassed by this. You are in a social studies class with a teacher who is not aware of your reading disability, and he asks you to read in front of the class from the text, which is written at the 10th-grade reading level. What do you do? How do you act? Your response will be determined in large part by your past school experiences. In the past, did you successfully engage in avoidance behaviors by being disruptive and being sent out of the room during instruction? Or were you taught a polite phrase to say, which you would follow up with a private conversation with the teacher? Or were you taught to be a self-advocate and to be proactive so the situation would not have occurred in the first place?

From a teacher's perspective, it is important to respond to such situations using the least dangerous assumption. The least dangerous assumption allows the teacher to assume the best and follow up later. In the case above, the teacher would assume that there is a perfectly reasonable explanation for the student's refusal to read aloud. This assumption is made regardless of the behavior the student displays. As a result of this assumption, the door is open for the teacher to initiate a personal conversation with the student.

Given that all behaviors serve a communicative intention, it becomes the responsibility of the team to

- Determine the communicative intent of the student's behaviors

- Assist the student in making the connection between his or her actions and feelings

- Support the student in learning alternative and efficient strategies to communicate his or her wants, needs, and desires

Once the communicative intent is identified, appropriate and supportive responses can follow.

As a team, it is important to talk about the challenges and frustrations that accompany the effort to understand the communicative intent of a student's behavior. This makes it more probable that adults will respond in responsible, empathic ways.

Power and Control Are Not Effective Ways to Shape Students' Behaviors

Imagine how a tiger reacts when forced into a corner. Typically, a trainer uses power and control to subdue the tiger. The trainer does this by moving toward the tiger, screaming, and snapping a whip. The tiger becomes angry and frightened, roars, and extends a leg in an attempt to push the trainer back. The trainer keeps pushing, screaming, and snapping the whip. The tiger has two choices. The first is to cower in the corner; the second is to lash out.

People are quite similar to tigers. When they are backed into a corner, either their spirits are broken and they cower or they lash out in response to feelings of fear and panic. Those who work with children and youth should not want to be the cause of such feelings. Using power and control to change a student's behavior is a way to back a student into a corner, and it is an inappropriate use of an adult's position. Teachers and paraprofessionals should not use power and control to manipulate a student into altering his or her challenging or unusual behaviors. Rather, the goal is to teach the student alternative ways to communicate his or her thoughts, needs, fears, and wishes. For some students, this process may take many years; this is why professional educators are responsible for designing PBS plans that are student centered and data based. Over time, the data provide the necessary information to determine whether the interventions are effective.

One way to determine if you or other members on your team use power and control is to listen to and watch your behaviors. Are team members using their physical size to threaten a student? During team meetings, do they describe the student as being noncompliant? Do you hear them raising their voices in anger? Yelling? Do they humiliate students by posting students' names on the board when they display behavior considered unacceptable? None of these adult behaviors should be allowed in your classroom if your intention is to create a safe classroom community. Para Form 18: Communicative Intent of Adult Behaviors (located in the Para Forms appendix) can help your team reflect on and analyze adult behaviors. When the adults in the classroom use predictable, proactive, positive behaviors, it increases the likelihood that students will respond accordingly. More importantly, the student behaviors that do emerge under these circumstances are the behaviors that the team truly needs to address.

Power and control are not specialized instructional supports. They are not effective in teaching students proactive, positive behaviors. When adults use these behaviors, students' behaviors do not change, adults do not feel better about their own professional lives, and ultimately a downward cycle is created for the students, teachers, and paraprofessionals.

Treat Students as You Would Like to Be Treated

Perhaps you have had a grandparent, parent, teacher, or wise elder in the community who taught you to treat others as you would like to be treated. I encourage you to take this lesson into the classroom. Think of a time recently when you were in emotional distress, a time when you felt angry, sad, or confused. How did you act? During that time, how did you want others to treat you? It is likely that you wanted kindness, support, and understanding. Perhaps you needed someone else to take care of you or to help you make decisions. It is likely that you did not want or need someone else to yell at you, lecture you, or punish you. Your feelings are similar to those of your students. When your students, especially those who experience challenging behaviors, are at their most vulnerable, treat them with the most care.

Together, these five tenets can guide your approach to determining the communicative intent of a student's behavior. When teachers, paraprofessionals, other school personnel, and family members operate from the same underlying assumptions, it increases the likelihood that they will understand the communicative intent of a student's behavior and that any interventions they choose will match that intent, be humane, and enhance the student's status. Such alignment assists team members in avoiding the blame game. You will begin to expend less energy on blaming a student for his or her behaviors and more time and energy trying to understand why the student is behaving in a certain manner and teaching more appropriate responses.

Reflection

Individually and as a team, evaluate your strengths related to the five tenets of positive behavior support. In which areas would you like to improve? How can you leverage your individual strengths in order to support the whole team in this area?

WHAT ARE THE FIVE PURPOSES OF BEHAVIORS?

After you have taken time to reflect on the meanings of the underlying tenets that fuel adult responses to behaviors, it is time to begin to understand the meanings of student-specific behaviors. The meaning of behaviors can be categorized into five specific areas (Durand, 1988; Evans & Meyer, 1985):

1. Seeking attention from someone

2. Avoiding or escaping a situation, task, person, or an event

3. Obtaining something tangible

4. Self-regulating energy output

5. Playing

The first three areas are related to communicating that the individual wants something from someone else.

Seeking Attention

The first purpose of behaviors is attention-seeking behaviors, which are used to communicate that an individual wants to engage in a social interaction with another person (e.g., conversation, acknowledgement, embrace). All human beings experience this need, and most people have a variety of socially acceptable verbal and nonverbal means of communicating this need. However, imagine if you had no traditional means of communicating this request efficiently and effectively. How would you tell someone you loved them? How could you ask if they loved you? How could you ask for a hug, a handshake, or a simple greeting? How would your attempts change over time (e.g., as a 4-year-old versus a 14-year-old)? Would you stop trying to communicate? Some unusual or challenging behaviors are simply attempts to get the attention of another person.

Classroom teachers need to be keenly aware of how each student with disabilities communicates the need for attention. To experience a sense of belonging, students with disabilities need the same type and frequency of interaction with the classroom teacher as do students without disabilities. Far too often, given the complexities of the classroom and the needs of every student, it is easy for classroom teachers to fall into the pattern of thinking "I am responsible for 30 students; the paraprofessional just has one student with disabilities, so it's easier for her to deal with the student." Although this may sound logical, Broer, Doyle, and Giangreco (2005) found that adults with disabilities described their lack of interaction with classroom teachers as being among the most painful experiences in their educational careers. One adult said, "The classroom teacher didn't know me very well" (p. 423). Another explained, "They told me that I couldn't get a teacher to help me because they're busy with other things in the room" (p. 423). A more appropriate approach to the needs, demands, and opportunities in the classroom is to have two adults responsible for and interacting with all students.

ACTIVITY 11

Attention Seeking

Each member of the team should take several opportunities to observe a student who has been identified as displaying challenging behaviors. Refer to Activity 10: Creating a Positive Atmosphere, located in the Activities appendix.

Compare your observations and answer these questions:

- Does this student have friends?

- Does this student have the skills to engage in conversations with peers?

- In what ways can we support the student in developing the skills necessary for friendships?

- How does the student get attention from others?

- Who gives that attention?

- Is the attention in the form of correction, teaching, or socialization?

Avoiding or Escaping a Situation, Task, Person, or an Event

The second purpose of behaviors is to communicate the need to escape or avoid a situation. With these behaviors, the sender intends to communicate that he or she is finished with an activity, wants to leave the situation, or wants a break. This is a critical communication skill for students, especially for those who communicate in nontraditional ways. The ability to communicate these needs is important for self-protection and self-regulation. Too often, teachers and paraprofessionals try to compel students to comply rather than respond to the student's communicative intent.

Obtaining Something Tangible

The third purpose of behaviors is to get something. A person may try to communicate that he or she wants food, a drink, desired items (e.g., toys, favorite clothes), or transportation. A person may also try to communicate that he or she does *not* want any of these things. Take a moment to imagine this in relationship to your own life. If you did not have a communication mode that was efficient or easily understood by others, how would you communicate that you wanted a specific book or food item? How would you make your own preferences known to others? If your communication attempts were not understood, how long would it take before you either lashed out in frustration or stopped trying to communicate?

Self-Regulation and Play

The last two purposes differ from the first three. Neither self-regulation nor play requires communicative responses from other people; both can be completely self-reinforcing behaviors. They are activities that a person finds pleasurable. For example, many people find the repetitive motion of a rocking chair to be quite calming. Others find playing a game of solitaire to be very relaxing. Because of people's inherent need to calm themselves and to have opportunities to engage in activities by themselves, it is very important to teach students with disabilities a variety of leisure activities that meet those needs. Some students with disabilities need to be taught how to use a rocking chair, a porch swing, or a compact disc player.

As with all students, it is important for students with disabilities to have lives that are filled with rich and interesting learning opportunities. Far too often, teams focus on managing behaviors first, and they do so in isolation. Instead, provide a rich and interesting curriculum with appropriate literacy demands and concurrently implement positive behavior supports. When your team determines that the communicative intent of a student's behavior is play or self-regulation, for example, do not try to extinguish the behavior; rather, teach an appropriate replacement behavior within a context of providing rich and interesting curriculum opportunities that link to the child's strengths.

1. Determine the communicative intent of the behavior via antecedent–behavior–consequence (A-B-C). As a teacher or paraprofessional, this will assist you in determining what triggers a behavior (antecedent) and what maintains it (consequence).

2. Conduct a schedule analysis to identify any patterns in the timing of behaviors. Use Para Form 19: Schedule Analysis (located in the Para Forms appendix).

To complete Para Form 19: Schedule Analysis, simply write the time a behavior occurred, identify the activity, and check off both the instructional format and teaching style. Finally, conduct a formal A-B-C. By conducting an A-B-C in the context of a schedule analysis, it is more likely that the team will be able to determine if there is a timely link.

This information will assist the team in deciding whether the student's behavior needs to be the primary focus or if adults need to change. The adults may need to discuss their own behaviors, perhaps whether there are mismatches in curriculum, schedule, or expectations. For example, a middle school student identified as having behavioral difficulties participated in a pull-out literacy lesson that focused on reading a children's book aloud. Immediately after leaving that pull-out lesson, she returned to the general education classroom, where the class was studying the American Revolution. Imagine the shift this required in terms of content, process, and literacy demands. It would have been more helpful if the pull-out time was used to support the literacy demands that were required for the social studies lesson. There was no ill intent on the part of any team member, simply a lack of communication and coordination. This observation of the student prompted the special educator on the team to begin the process of addressing how the team could better serve their students.

Reflection

What is the relationship between pull-out classes and classroom content? How are students supported in making the physical and curricular shift from a pull-out or self-contained class to the general education class?

HOW SHOULD WE ADDRESS CHALLENGING BEHAVIORS?

When a student exhibits challenging behaviors, the education team may follow several steps to address and change the behaviors:

1. Examine your own teaching practices.

2. Identify the student's relationships with peers.

3. Compare the literacy demands of the instructional materials with the student's literacy level.

4. Make a logical guess about the purpose of the student's behaviors, and test the guess with data collection.

5. Identify the communicative intent of the behaviors.

6. Design a PBS plan that outlines the behavior that is being changed, the communicative intent of that behavior, a specific replacement behavior for the student, appropriate intervention strategies, and the data collection strategies.

Examine Your Teaching

Prior to engaging in a full scale examination of issues related to the student, it is always advisable to examine the behaviors of the adults on the classroom team at the time of the unusual, disruptive, or disturbing behavior. It is not unusual for the behavior to be a result of inconsistency in instructions or routines on the part of the teacher or paraprofessional. The teacher may be saying one thing and the paraprofessional something different to the same student. One way to examine the relationship between the adults' behaviors and the student's reactions is to use the A-B-C observational format.

Another common difficulty is during transitions between separate classroom activities. If a transition is unclear or unusually chaotic, the teacher should calmly interrupt the transition and assist the students in regrouping by saying, "I'm sorry, I left out part of the directions for this transition, so I would like to back up and give you the instructions once again. Ready? Refer to your schedules and, using inside voices, gather your pencil and reading materials for reading group. Now walk quietly to your groups."

Yet another area of teaching to examine is the frequency with which the teacher engages with the student 1) with positive energy and input and 2) in a manner that communicates that the teacher knows that the student is smart and capable of doing rich and interesting work.

Identify the Student's Relationships with Peers

A common area of difficulty for students is friendships and socialization. If a problem is suspected, the teacher or paraprofessional should collect very specific data about the student's social connections with peers and adults. Examination of frequency, duration, and quality of interactions can be very helpful to the team.

Table 5.1 displays details about Sarah's interactions with her teacher and paraprofessional. The student, Sarah, has been yelling at her classmates both in and out of class. Her paraprofessional does not know what will trigger her. The least intrusive approach to analyzing this interaction would be to examine the teacher's instructional practice and to modify that practice when appropriate. This needs to be followed up by supporting Sarah in building relationships with her peers. Helping students establish friendships requires ongoing support and intervention, but the adults could begin by having Sarah participate in shared activities in a small group of three to five peers. The team should identify Sarah's strengths and how they can be leveraged in a peer group. The team will also need to identify the types of support she might need. Keep in mind that ongoing opportunities to participate in shared activities increase the likelihood that friendships will develop.

Compare the Literacy Demands of the Instructional Materials

A mismatch in literacy demands in any subject area is another common area of difficulty for middle and high school students. If the student reads at the third-grade level and he or she is in a 10th-grade social studies class, the frustration and embarrassment that emerges over time can be significant. The classroom teacher and special educator need to work together in advance of these situations to ensure that every student has opportunities to engage in rich and interesting curriculum and to use written materials at his or her skill level. For example, in a high school English class the students are reading Shakespeare's plays during their junior year. Traditionally, available texts are either written at that level or are read in the original text by advanced students. Karen, who has Down syndrome, reads at the third-grade level. She follows along when students read the plays aloud in class but

Table 5.1. Identifying interaction contexts for Sarah

Date and time	Interaction partner	Responds to interaction	Purpose of interaction
10/17 10:00	Paraprofessional	Yelled at paraprofessional	Paraprofessional told her to get on task.
10/18 10:30	Teacher	Huffed and slammed books on desk	Teacher asked for her homework for the second time.
10/21 10:15	Teacher	Slammed books and put head on desk	Teacher directed her to get to work.

Initial patterns

1. All interactions are with adults.
   a. Follow-up questions: Does Sarah have friends? Does she interact with peers?
2. All interactions are in response to verbal requests from adults.
   a. Follow-up thoughts: Does Sarah use a personal to-do list during class? Might an increase in gestural cues and a decrease in verbal cues be helpful?
   b. Do the assignments match Sarah's literacy levels?

does not read the text aloud in class. She does, however, prepare for class in the following ways:

- During speech therapy, she reviews related vocabulary using an online flashcard program.

- In her first-period study hall she receives individual support from a paraprofessional in the library, where they read from *Streamlined Shakespeare,* a version of the play being read in class that is written at the third-grade reading level. They also review the vocabulary flashcards using an online flashcard program.

- After school, Karen reviews the flashcards as the homework and watches the movie.

There is no doubt in anyone's mind that Karen is well versed in the life of William Shakespeare and specifically the plays *Romeo and Juliet* and *Macbeth.* Prior to the use of these types of materials, she was disengaged and bored during class because the texts were so foreign to her. As a way to self-manage her boredom, she engaged in behaviors that disrupted the class. Karen did not need a behavior program; rather, she needed the curricular materials to be adapted to address her literacy needs. Please note that several web sites that host reading materials of high-interest and low-readability levels are identified in Chapter 4.

Make a Logical Guess and Test It Out

When a team is trying to determine the communicative intent of a student's behaviors, it is helpful to begin with an examination of each of the five purposes of behaviors discussed previously: attention, avoidance, obtaining of something tangible, self-regulation, and play (Durand, 1988; Evans & Meyer, 1985). Teams begin by making logical guesses about the purpose of a particular behavior and then test the guess by collecting data. Often, the actual communicative intent of a student's unusual, disturbing, or distracting behavior can be identified through this method, and a more effective and acceptable strategy can be taught to the student.

To determine the communicative intent of a student's behavior, members of the team need to observe the student and record what they see, what they hear, and the circumstances in which the behavior is occurring. It is important to remember that although a paraprofessional can (and should) assist with gathering observational data, it is not the paraprofessional's responsibility to interpret the behavior or to design the intervention approach that will be used. Designing the observation method is the responsibility of licensed personnel. Para Form 20: Determining Communicative Intent via Antecedent–Behavior–Consequence (a blank version of this form appears in the Para Forms appendix) provides team members with a structure to use in beginning this process. Each team member who works with the student should take the responsibility to conduct observations so that a more complete picture can be drawn of the student's behaviors across time, people (e.g., while with peers, paraprofessional, teachers, therapists), and places (e.g., classroom, cafeteria, playground).

Typically, it is the special educator's responsibility to train the general educator, paraprofessional, and related services personnel how to use specific observational techniques.

One way to initiate this training is to introduce and explain the Determining Communicative Intent para form at a team meeting. Have team members study the form. Share an example of a form completed by the special educator in reference to the student and the specific behavior in question. (It would be helpful if the special educator had a videotape to accompany the example.) Then, team members can practice using the form while monitoring students on the playground, in the cafeteria, during instruction, or anywhere students congregate. Keep in mind that the team should be using the form for a specified behavior; otherwise, team members will end up observing every little detail of the student's behaviors. Finally, the special educator should ensure that each relevant member of the team has two or three opportunities to observe the student for specific periods of time. This might entail shifting roles for temporary periods of time. For example, the general education teacher may need the special educator to teach the class for a time while he or she observes the student. During the time the paraprofessional observes the student, someone else may have to provide student support. After each member of the team has had several opportunities to observe the student, the team should meet to interpret the data (i.e., their observation recordings). The team's goal is to examine the data and determine the communicative intent of the student's behavior. The special educator then designs a positive behavior support plan based on the communicative intent, intensity of the behavior, and frequency of the behavior and incorporates the student's strengths and needs.

An element of this training that should not be overlooked is the ability to use these techniques with all students in the classroom. As team members become skillful with different ways of determining the communicative intent of behaviors, it is likely that they will use the same approaches with students without disabilities. Middle and high school teachers may find these approaches to be especially helpful.

Identify the Communicative Intent of Behaviors

One strategy that is often used to help understand behavior is an A-B-C analysis, as was briefly described previously. The *antecedent* is the event that occurs immediately before a specific behavior, often triggering the behavior. The *behavior* is the specific unusual or disruptive action that can be seen or heard. The *consequence* is what happens immediately after the behavior and functions to maintain or reinforce the behavior. Using an A-B-C analysis, you can identify what triggers and maintains a behavior (see Figure 5.1 for a filled-out example of Para Form 20: Determining Communicative Intent via Antecedent–Behavior–Consequence; a blank version of this form appears in the Para Forms appendix).

Actually, many parents learn this cycle quickly. For example, a father holds his toddler up in the air (A = antecedent); the toddler giggles, laughs, and breathes hard (B = behavior); and the father sets the toddler down (C = consequence). The father quickly learns that if he holds his toddler in the air (A), then the child will giggle, laugh, and breathe hard (B). When put down (C), the toddler calms down enough to breathe regularly again. The father thus learns to put his toddler down when the child gets too excited. Typical daily routines and experiences can be viewed through an A-B-C framework.

When children or youth display challenging behaviors, the team may find it helpful to gather several A-B-Cs across people, times, and locations to determine what may be trig-

Figure 5.1

Determining Communicative Intent via Antecedent–Behavior–Consequence

Antecedent	Behavior	Consequence
What happened immediately before the difficult behavior occurred?	Describe what you heard and saw.	What happened immediately after the behavior?
Paraprofessional says, "It's your turn to read, Sam."	Sam says "I don't want to read."	Silence; students in the group wait for Sam to read.
Paraprofessional states more firmly, "Sam, it is your turn to read. We're all waiting for you."	Sam refuses and says, "I don't want to."	Paraprofessional's voice become more firm. "Everyone has to take a turn, and we're all going to just sit here and wait for you." All students are out of instruction.
	Sam screams, "I said I'm not reading!" He stands up, throws his chair, and leaves the group.	Paraprofessional appears angry and tells Sam, "That's it. I'm getting Mrs. Sparks (classroom teacher) to deal with you." Remaining students are still out of instruction.

Communicative intent:	Interpretation:
☐ Attention seeking ☑ Escape or avoidance ☐ Obtaining something tangible ☐ Self-regulation ☐ Play	Sam is trying to get out of an uncomfortable situation. There needs to be a better way for him to practice reading without becoming embarrassed. Given his reading level (i.e., lower than his peers), the current approach of trying to force him to read in a group is inappropriate and unproductive for everyone. Alternatives to this situation will be discussed during the next team meeting. Additional training needs to occur at the team level to teach the paraprofessional to 1) recognize the signs of student stress that are likely to result in an undesirable outcome and 2) respond with an appropriate intervention.

Figure 5.1. Example of Para Form 20: Determining Communicative Intent via Antecedent-Behavior-Consequence.

gering and maintaining the behaviors. Take a moment to recall the five purposes of behavior (attention seeking, avoidance, obtaining of something tangible, self-regulation, and play). Now return to Figure 5.1 and examine the observational data shown there, which describes Sam, a second-grade student. What is your hunch about the communicative intent of Sam's behavior? His education team would likely determine that his communicative intent is escape or avoidance of reading class. On the basis of this interpretation, the intervention would be very different from an intervention based on a preliminary guess that Sam's behavior indicates that he is seeking play or attention. Clearly, Sam's team needs to develop a plan to 1) understand why he wants to avoid reading class and 2) remedy that situation.

HOW DO WE DESIGN A POSTIVE BEHAVIOR SUPPORT PLAN?

Once the communicative intent of a student's behavior has been identified, the special educator can lead the team in designing a PBS plan that can be implemented by each member of the team (*Note:* It is never appropriate for the paraprofessional to design the PBS plan). This plan should include

1. The communicative intent of the student's behavior

2. A clear description of the behavior that is being changed, reduced, or eliminated

3. A specific replacement behavior that is being taught to the student

4. Appropriate instructional strategies

5. Data collection strategies

Figure 5.2 offers one example of how the special educator can document the PBS plan for other team members. It is important that each member of the team understand that it is not enough simply to identify the behavior that needs to be reduced or eliminated. Identifying and teaching a replacement behavior, which is a substitute for the unacceptable

Description of the target behavior that you are trying to eliminate:		
Description of the target behavior that you are trying to teach:		
Communicative intent of the behavior that you are trying to eliminate:		
Prevent	**Teach**	**Respond**
In what ways will you prevent the target behavior from occurring?	How will you teach the replacement behavior?	How will you respond to the new behavior? What if the target behavior occurs again?
Strategy 1		
Strategy 2		
Strategy 3		

Figure 5.2. Positive behavior support plan for team members.

behavior, are key to success with the student. The replacement behavior becomes the primary focus. It needs to serve the same function for the student yet be

- Easier to perform or access than the original behavior

- More effective and efficient than the original behavior

- More reinforcing than the original behavior

Often, when students are identified as needing behavioral supports, the educational team uses much of the information in the chapter to develop a written PBS plan. A licensed member of the teaching team (e.g., special educator, general educator, psychologist) takes the lead with this responsibility. Every member of the team has a responsibility to be familiar with and implement the plan. This plan should clearly describe the behavior that is to be changed, the communicative function of that behavior, and the replacement behavior.

It is also helpful if the written plan identifies ways to use the student's strengths and interests as points of leverage while the student is learning the replacement behavior. The PBS example shown in Figure 5.3 presents another way to document the plan for all team members. This plan is rooted in the five tenets of PBS and uses the framework of understanding the communicative intent of the behavior well enough that the team will work to prevent the behavior, teach alternative responses, and respond in a consistent manner if the behavior does occur. Review and discuss the elements of the form with your team. Answer these questions: Would this be helpful for any of our students? Is the form we are already using just as effective?

Positive behavior support plan			
Name: _____ Activity/Class: _____ Teacher(s): _____			

Student's strengths (i.e., can-do behaviors)		Student's interests	
☆ ☆ ☆ ☆ ☆		☆ ☆ ☆ ☆ ☆	

Student supports for prevention	Challenging behavior	Replacement behavior	If individual instructional materials are necessary, who will develop the materials?
	Communicative intent		Who will support the teacher to implement the plan?
	Response when behavior occurs	How to teach the replacement behavior	Other relevant skills

Figure 5.3. Positive behavior support plan. (From Hedeen, D., & Ayers, B. [1998, November]. *Positive behavior support plan.* Paper presented at the meeting of The Associations for Persons with Severe Handicaps, Seattle, WA.; adapted by permission.)

Some teams will find it helpful to explicitly state the paraprofessional's responsibilities for supporting and encouraging positive behaviors among all students in the classroom. As your team reads this chapter, engage in the discussion points throughout. Be open, clear, and direct. Discuss the questions and reflections sprinkled throughout this chapter, as they are designed to support your team in going beyond tasks and responsibilities to develop a deeper awareness, respect, and regard for one another. It is very important that the team members, especially the general educator, special educator, and paraprofessional, support one another by actively communicating about students who demonstrate challenging behavior. The day-to-day realities of supporting these students can be very wearing. The checklist shown in Figure 5.4 lists the most common proactive and reactive duties related to positive behavior supports and will help to ensure that you are working together. Using the blank copy of this checklist, complete it as a team. Para Form 21: Responsibilities Related to Encouraging Positive Classroom Behaviors is located in the Para Forms appendix.

Paraprofessional Self-Advocacy

Ask the other team members to update you on any students who require PBS plans by describing the disruptive behavior. Team members should explain the communicative intent of that behavior, identify the replacement behavior, and demonstrate any interventions that you are expected to implement.

If you support a student with challenging behaviors, use the prompts on Para Form 3: Advocacy Skills for Paraprofessionals: Asking for What You Need (located in the Para Forms appendix) as a guide to ask for what you need from the special education teacher.

HOW DO WE IMPLEMENT A POSITIVE BEHAVIOR SUPPORT PLAN?

Many paraprofessionals are responsible for providing individual or small-group instruction designed by the classroom teacher or the special educator. A paraprofessional can use several strategies, with minimal management of behavior, to increase the likelihood that students will remain engaged: foster a supportive classroom atmosphere, develop consistent reminders of positive behaviors, offer choices to students, use planned ignoring, and maintain focus on the communicative intent.

Foster a Positive Classroom Atmosphere

Establishing an atmosphere that is generally positive, predictable, and consistent is the first step in supporting all students. Many strategies do not generally require the approval of a certified teacher. For instance, the paraprofessional can do the following:

- Be prepared with all of the necessary teaching materials before the students arrive.

- Welcome each student warmly and greet each student by name and with a smile as a kind invitation into instruction.

- Avoid too many yes or no questions during the instruction; instead, offer students choices and opportunities to express their ideas. This gives students a sense of control and contribution. It also encourages students to engage in complex thinking.

Responsibilities Related to Encouraging Positive Classroom Behaviors

Responsibilities	General or special educator	Paraprofessional
Establish class routines, expectations, and/or rules.	X	
Schedule class activities and daily/weekly schedule.	X	
Establish behavioral goals for individuals or groups of students.	X	
Write the positive behavior support plan, including target behavior to increase (replacement behavior), target behavior to decrease, instructional plan to teach the replacement behavior, reinforcement and reinforcement schedule, consequences for/responses to not demonstrating appropriate behavior, data collection system, review of data.	X	
Train the paraprofessional to implement the positive behavior support plan.	X	
Observe and provide feedback on the paraprofessional's implementation.	X	
Implement general classroom routines, expectations, and/or rules.	X	X
Implement individual behavior support plans.	X	X
Collect appropriate data.	X	X
Evaluate the effectiveness of classroom routines, expectations, and/or rules.	X	
Evaluate the effectiveness of individual positive behavior support plans.	X	
Use evaluation data to alter plans.	X	

Figure 5.4. Example of Para Form 21: Responsibilities Related to Encouraging Positive Classroom Behaviors.

- Avoid repeating verbal cues that can come across as nagging. If a student does not respond to a request, it is likely that he or she heard it but is choosing not to respond. Restate the expectation once, giving the student a specific and reasonable time frame. Then let it go. If the student responds, acknowledge the response in a positive manner without expressing excitement. If he or she does not respond, make a note of it. Work with the teacher to determine the communicative intent of the student's behavior and design an appropriate and supportive intervention.

- Be consistent in teaching PBS plans; children and youth rely on the adults in their world to be consistent.

- Avoid threats, bribes, lectures, and power struggles. They are not forms of specialized instruction.

- Implement any individualized PBS plans, keeping the five tenets of PBS in mind.

- Ask for help and feedback frequently.

- Remember that most students really do want to have a positive school experience. Encourage each student and communicate very explicitly pleasure at having him or her in the group.

- Always assume that all students want to do what is right.

- Allow students to save face. This increases the likelihood that they will learn the intended lesson. Humiliation, power, and control are never effective teaching methods.

- Be aware of own attitudes and feelings prior to entering the classroom each day. Bring a sense of energy and optimism.

- Apologize to a student for making a mistake or speaking in a harsh manner. Be specific with the apology by naming the behavior and accompanying feelings: "Cathy, I'm really sorry that I used a harsh tone of voice with you. That tone isn't helpful. It must have been hurtful to you."

These strategies go a long way in creating a supportive learning environment. It can be helpful for the classroom teacher and the paraprofessional to review these steps frequently, perhaps even posting them in the instructional space.

Develop Consistent Reminders of Positive Behaviors

Many students (and adults, for that matter) find comfort in knowing that the atmosphere and expectations of the classroom are consistently positive and clear. Any adult in the classroom can support individual students with cues. Start with nonintrusive cuing strategies, and move to more intrusive strategies only as needed. Table 5.2 lists both the strategies and the examples. As a team, discuss explicitly how and under what circumstances the paraprofessional should use each of these strategies with individual students or with all students.

These cuing strategies offer gentle reminders to students about maintaining positive behaviors. Some students may need team members to consistently use one specific strategy. In such cases, the teacher should both show and tell the paraprofessional how and under what circumstances to use the strategy.

Offer Choices to Students

Keep in mind that practice makes perfect. The more a student engages in positive behaviors and receives positive consequences, the more likely it is that the student will learn and maintain a cycle of positive behavior. It becomes your responsibility to structure the classroom environment in such a way that all students experience that cycle often. One way to do this is to frequently offer students choice-making opportunities throughout their daily

Table 5.2. Nonintrusive behavioral support strategies

Strategy	Examples
State the expectation	Tell students what to do and how you want them to do it.
Use proximity	Stand closer to the student who is engaged in inappropriate behavior. Do not look at the student. Instead, keep your focus on the teaching at hand.
Use a gentle touch	Touch the student's shoulder or arm while maintaining focus on the instruction at hand.
Give nonverbal cues	Smile, nod, or give a thumbs-up to reinforce appropriate behaviors.
Give indirect verbal cues	Make a statement about the behaviors of another student. For example, when a student calls out an answer, say, "I like the way Sue is raising her hand."
Give direct verbal cues	In a quiet and private manner, tell the student exactly how you want him or her to behave. End the statement by saying, "Thank you." Step away from the student. During the interaction, act calm and dispassionate, regardless of how you actually feel.
Offer a choice	Offer the student a choice in which the options are incompatible with continuing the behavior. For example, when a student refuses to do an assignment that requires writing, you could ask, "Do you want to use a black pen or a purple pen to do the assignment?" or "Do you want to sit at your desk or at the table to do this project?"

Table 5.3. Chioce-making opportunities

Types of choice	Examples
Within an activity: A choice of two or more materials in which the choice is provided within the context of the activity	*Reading:* Choose the book from two options *Math:* Choose the manipulatives *Lunch:* Choose the dessert
Between activities: A choice between two or more activities	Reading or math Math worksheet or manipulatives
Refusal: At the beginning of an activity, a choice of whether to participate in the activity	*Science:* "You must participate in the experiment. You can choose whether to write up the lab."
Who: A choice of which classmate the student wants to participate with	Choose a partner Choose which student's notes to photocopy Choose which student to walk with from the bus to the classroom
Where: A choice among two or more places for the activity to occur	*Reading:* "Do you want to do this activity in the classroom, the library, or in the resource room?"
When: A choice of when the activity occurs	*Morning activities:* "Do you want to do math or reading first?" *Art:* "Would you rather paint or sculpt first?"
Terminate: A choice of ending the activity at a self-selected time	"Signal when you are finished."

Source: Brown, Belz, Corsi, and Wenig (1993).

activities (see Table 5.3). The ability to make a choice gives students a certain degree of control over their daily lives.

Offering students choices rather than trying to control their behaviors can be an important aspect of instruction. When offering a choice to a student, be certain that it really is a choice. For example, if a third-grade student refuses to participate in math activities, it would be inappropriate to say, "Do your work or go home," because going home is not really a choice. It would be more productive and positive to say, "Would you like to do your math problems or listen to the book on tape first?" In the second example, both items are legitimate choices. The student needs to do both, but the order is less important.

You might also pair options that require very different types of energy from the student: "Would you like to do the math problems or work on the geometric structure first?" Again, both choices are tasks that need to be completed, but you are giving the student control over the order. You are also teaching the student how to match his or her energy level with an option. Adults generally understand the need to match their energy levels with the tasks that need to be accomplished on a daily basis. For example, you may have to vacuum the floor and write a letter to a friend today. In the morning, when you are feeling refreshed and quiet, you might choose to write the letter. As the day becomes noisier and busier, you might be more likely to vacuum the floor. Allowing students to make a choice about which activity they want to pursue gives them practice in matching their energy levels to their activities and helps them fine-tune this skill.

Use Planned Ignoring

One strategy often used to alter behavior is planned ignoring. Planned ignoring refers to the complete inattention or lack of acknowledgment of an identified behavior. The identified behavior is the behavior that the team has decided interferes with the student's learning and growth. When planned ignoring is called for (as defined in the student's individualized PBS plan), the team members, including the paraprofessional, should observe the following guidelines (Doyle, 2002):

1. Offer no acknowledgment of the behavior. Do not look at, speak to, or cue the student about the behavior.

2. Be consistent.

3. Act as if the behavior is not occurring at all. Offer no positive or negative attention.

4. Generously praise students who are behaving in an appropriate manner. Make the praise specific to those behaviors that are incompatible with the target behavior. For example, if the student refuses to raise his or her hand, say to another student, "Sara, thanks for raising your hand. What did you want to say?" Do not say, "Carl, look at Sara raising her hand. If you do that, I will call on you."

5. Be very consistent.

6. Catch the student doing the right thing. Respond immediately to the first demonstration of the desired behavior that you see. For example, when Carl raises his hand, call on him for a response. Praise him.

7. Be very, very consistent.

8. Do not lecture or discuss the behavior with the student.

9. Discuss the information and experiences with the classroom teacher and the special educator.

10. Be very, very, very consistent.

Teaching team members how and when to ignore a student's behavior is very important. Planned ignoring is a difficult skill to learn because it is so easy to develop a cycle of reacting to a behavior or set of behaviors instead of teaching a student alternative responses. What makes planned ignoring so effective, however, is that it disrupts the student's attempt to communicate using the target behavior, and it encourages the student to shift to the new, more effective behavior. Remember, it is ultimately the responsibility of the certified team members to decide when and under what circumstances planned ignoring should be used.

Maintain Focus on the Communicative Intent

It often takes time for students to learn replacement behaviors that are as powerful and effective as the original, unusual, disruptive, or challenging behaviors. Consistency on the part of adults is critical. One way to support the adults (e.g., classroom teacher, paraprofessional) in being consistent as they teach the student alternative responses is to use a reminder system, such as that shown in Table 5.4. This was created to help the adults working with a student, Sara, remember the actual reasons behind Sara's behavior so they could avoid unproductive responses to her behaviors.

Table 5.4. Reminder: Fun facts about Sara

Fact: What Sara might do	Myths and misinterpretations	What Sara is actually trying to say
Grabbing another student by the shoulder	Sara is trying to hurt the other student.	"I want to play/work with you."
Giving a short scream followed by throwing materials	Sara is trying to avoid work. She is lazy. She is unwilling to work.	"This is too hard. I don't understand what you are asking me to do."
Pulling long hair	Sara is being mean.	"I like you. Please pay attention to me."

Clearly, adults and peers can significantly change their responses to challenging behavior when they understand the student's true communicative intent. When the team is trying to teach a student replacement behaviors, it is important that those behaviors are easier to do and more powerful than the student's original behavior.

Paraprofessional Self-Advocacy

To clarify your responsibilities for supporting students in developing appropriate behavior, ask team members for the following:

1. Clarification about your responsibilities in the classroom for supporting all students in maintaining appropriate behavior. Ask specific questions. For example, you might ask, "If I notice students without disabilities passing notes or speaking out, how would you like me to respond?"

2. Clarification about how both you and the classroom teacher will take responsibility for students' individual PBS plans. Who will collect the data?

3. Modeling interventions that are listed on any individual PBS plans. This modeling should be done by the special educator and take place in the same settings in which you will implement the plan. This should be followed up with a request for the special educator to observe you and give you feedback on your implementation.

CONCLUSION

Implementing the suggestions in this chapter and responding to paraprofessionals' training requests will result in a much stronger teaching team. These types of interactions increase the skill base that is needed to support, encourage, and teach students who experience a range of needs. They also encourage a level of discussion that is professional and responsible.

Supporting students whose behavior is unusual, disruptive, or challenging is important work. The five tenets of PBS along with the very basic intervention strategies that have been outlined in this chapter are meant to support teams in learning how to determine the communicative intent of a student's behavior. People acts in ways that communicate their experiences of the world. When their behaviors are unusual, disruptive, or challenging in some way, it is likely that they would prefer that those around them try to understand and respond rather than punish them and push them away. The children and youth you work with deserve the same regard and respect. As adults, it is your ethical responsibility to act with kindness and respect toward *all* children and youth.

6

Maintaining Confidentiality

Objectives

- Develop proactive systems of communication among adults
- Develop a system to communicate specialized instruction
- Understand the importance of maintaining student and family confidentiality
- Learn guidelines for supporting student privacy

General and special educators, paraprofessionals, and extended members of the education team need to be able to communicate about many things. At a minimum, team members need to communicate about issues related to IEPs, curriculum planning and support, role clarification, and scheduling. Communication is the foundation of effective teamwork. Your team needs to decide on both the frequency and type of communication strategies that will be most effective in your circumstances. The general or special educator on the team may already have formal or informal strategies to facilitate communication among team members. The paraprofessional needs to understand how he or she fits into the communication loop. Of particular importance is how the entire team communicates on a regular basis about individual student programming needs.

Para Form 22: Team Communication, located in the Para Forms appendix, provides an opportunity to clarify each team member's role and responsibility in developing effective communication strategies. As a team, first discuss and identify when team meetings should be scheduled. Then, identify the topics that will be addressed during those meetings. Finally, discuss and identify team members who need to be involved in discussions related to each of the identified topics. Keep in mind that it is not necessary for everyone to be at every meeting. If your team can identify those members whose presence is most important and how you can get input from the others in an efficient manner, you free up time for all team members to spend teaching and supporting students.

If your team has not discussed communication strategies, use the Team Communication para form as a way to approach the topic. Whatever strategies your classroom-based team uses, communication between teachers and paraprofessionals must occur on a weekly or biweekly basis and in ways that are clear and efficient. There may be some items the team decides can be handled via e-mail or password-protected discussion forum, but ongoing communication is a must. When communicating via e-mail about students, keep in mind that confidentiality must be maintained and that because parents are members of the team, they too need to be aware of communications concerning their child. It is a good idea to print a copy of any such communication for the student's file. Before sending something in writing about a student or the student's family, ask yourself the following questions:

1. What is my intention?

2. If I knew the student's parents were going to read this right now, would I say the same things?

3. Should I copy the parents on the e-mail as a courtesy?

4. Is there anything in this e-mail that could be misunderstood?

5. Have I abided by the school's confidentiality policies?

In answering these questions, team members will be more aware of the language they choose to describe situations. Regular, appropriate communication not only minimizes the likelihood of misunderstandings among team members but also maximizes the potential for proactive, effective problem solving and support.

Many teams also record minutes and take notes on the outcome of discussions during their meetings. Para Form 23: Meeting Agenda, located in the Para Forms appendix, is one method of recording important information in a way that is organized and easy to use.

Even with proactive communication systems, some situations require that paraprofessionals think and act quickly without the opportunity for discussions with licensed team members. When these situations arise, the paraprofessional should make the most appropriate decision based on the student's background and the specific circumstances. Para Form 24: Documenting Spontaneous Incidents, located in the Para Forms appendix, is a helpful way for the paraprofessional to document relevant information about specific incidents. The paraprofessional's documentation will provide important data for the team to reflect on in determining why the incident occurred and the most appropriate action to take in the future.

A Paraprofessional's Reflection

Over the years I have learned that clear and direct communication is a very important part of developing a healthy team. However, I've also learned that it takes work to get there. Every year the special educator I work with reviews the confidentiality policy of our school. She takes this responsibility very seriously and brings home the importance of it by explaining, "This stuff really is important. Parents trust us not only with their kids, but also with family information. Think about the amount of information that we have about their lives, but they don't have about ours. Or think about the numbers of details that we know about these kids' lives that we don't know about the lives of students without disabilities. It's a lot. Aspects of special education can be pretty intrusive, so we need to be incredibly respectful." Each year when she says that, it reminds me of why confidentiality is so important.

On a practical note, we do meet as a classroom team about twice a month for 30 minutes. These meetings are preplanned and very focused, with a written agenda. We solve problems individual students might be having and assign responsibilities for upcoming units of instruction. Often we generate a to-do list for to the unit we're studying. Generally, the list includes materials that need to be gathered, made, or adapted. This approach gives everyone a heads-up about when things need to be done. We don't waste any time!

Paraprofessional Self-Advocacy

If your team does not have a regularly scheduled meeting to discuss students' curricular and instructional needs, ask the special educator, "Can we schedule regular meetings so I know what I need to focus on with students [i.e., instructional goals] and how I should do it [i.e., instructional strategies]?"

When a meeting is scheduled, bring Para Form 3: Advocacy Skills for Paraprofessionals: Asking for What You Need worksheet (located in the Para Forms appendix) to be certain you understand the level of specificity needed to support the teachers as they design specialized instruction. This form can serve as a prompt to the teachers so that no one falls into the trap of assuming that you will just "figure it out."

SPECIALIZED INSTRUCTION

This book repeatedly states that certified personnel (i.e., classroom teachers, special educators, therapists) are responsible for designing, implementing, and evaluating instruction. It is also their responsibility to train and supervise the paraprofessional and evaluate his or her implementation of the instruction. Often, the certified personnel have many students on their caseloads who require different instructional approaches. Organizing this information is a very important responsibility. At Richmond Elementary School in Richmond, Vermont, the special educator, Mrs. Cobb, recognizes how important it is to give paraprofessionals on her team clear, organized information. Her strategy (see Table 6.1) is to list several of the student's IEP goals, the instructional strategies to be used, and data collection strategies.

Mrs. Cobb uses this format each time she works with the paraprofessional and classroom teacher to write down what a student will learn and how the adults will ensure that they provide the appropriate instruction. The classroom teacher and paraprofessional review the Instructional Strategies column, in particular, and ask any questions about training and support. Then, Mrs. Cobb provides direct instruction to the classroom teacher and paraprofessional in the general education classroom. Each time the team meets to discuss issues of curriculum and instruction, this form is used as the core of the discussion and planning. Related services providers are expected to bring information that will sup-

Table 6.1. Example of organization of a student's individualized education program (IEP) goals

Mary's IEP goals	Instructional strategies	Data or evidence
Mary will learn three new thematic vocabulary words per classroom unit.	Flash cards, reading books related to the thematic topic, paraprofessional retells stories	Record word use in in home–school journal, science journal, reading response journal, bug body parts project; share data sheets containing words and facts
Mary will use her knowledge of sight words to read words in context and in isolation.	Flash cards, skywriting, red words, match-to-example activity	Date sheets and home–school journal
Mary will independently manage her personal belongings.	Picture schedule plus gestural prompts (that will be faded with time), daily review of schedule	Observations, videotape

port the team in teaching the student to move toward his or her IEP goals. For the education team, this translates into an explicit focus on the second column in particular.

The transition to middle and high school is important for the teaching staff to consider. This transition requires that the instructional priorities and strategies become more sophisticated. In the elementary example presented in Table 6.1, although the student may have the same goal of reading words as she moves to the middle school, the instructional approaches may differ. Rather than use skywriting or traditional flashcards, Mary might learn to use word prediction software or electronic flashcards. Teachers in the middle and high school may also actively use the voice output feature available through Microsoft Word and Adobe Acrobat. Using any type of assistive technology will require training for the teachers and paraprofessionals to ensure ease of use.

REMEMBERING THE GOALS OF MANY STUDENTS

It is not unusual for classroom teachers and paraprofessionals to ask, "How will I remember the goals and objectives of each of my students?" One strategy is to develop a master list like the one in Table 6.2. This helps the teacher, paraprofessional, and special educator focus on the needs of every child in the classroom. This type of matrix provides classroom personnel with a class list at a glance. Although it does not include a lot of detail, it does show the big picture.

Remembering individual instructional goals and strategies can become a bit more complex at the high school level. General education classroom teachers often have 100–125 students per week. Although the overall proportion of students with disabilities remains the same, 10%–12% (U.S. Department of Education, 2000), the numbers of individual students a teacher has across all of his or her classes is higher. High school teachers and paraprofessionals need a system that accommodates these larger numbers. In one area high school, the special education teachers develop matrices per subject area and class. Class lists are generated in a matrix (e.g., Excel spreadsheet). The students who receive special sup-

Table 6.2. Example of a master list of students and their instructional goals

	Extended time	Fewer problems	Curriculum overlapping	Multilevel instruction	Personal support
John	Double the time for tests				
Marta		Allow Marta to choose any five problems			Peer tutor
Sam			Initiating communication using picture symbols; finding his own desk using black adhesive dot on the right corner of his desk		Peer tutor
Balin				Accelerated math (algebra)	

ports are identified along with services, goals, and strategies that are relevant to specific classes (see Figure 6.1). In addition, some general education classroom teachers adapt this matrix so that it can be used more universally. They add notes on specific needs of all of the students in the class as well as a column in which they can document contacts they make with the students' families.

All student information is confidential. It is likely that the paraprofessional will need this information and therefore should be instructed where to keep it and how to use it. Information that the classroom teacher needs to know but the paraprofessional does not should be deleted from the paraprofessional's copy. One way to keep the copies straight is to color-code the paper (e.g., yellow is always for paraprofessionals and blue is always for classroom teachers). The paraprofessional should have a locked space in the classroom (e.g., filing cabinet drawer or desk drawer) where he or she can store the information. Maintaining a system like this is another way to improve communication among team members.

Accommodations Matrix

Class: Biology   Teacher: Ms. Payne   Period: 6th

	Check for understanding, repeat the directions, explain the task in another way	Graphic organizers	Control amount of work	Schedules, agendas, calendars, checklists, to-do lists, homework logs	Review systems, note-taking strategies	Visuals— electronic flashcards	Behavior contract	Communication with parents
Students and case managers								
Evan (504) MP	X			X	X	X		1x/month e-mail
Sasha (IEP) MP	X	X				X		1x/month e-mail
Karl (IEP) MP		X	X	X			X	2x/month phone
Chris (IEP) CK	X			X		X		1x/month e-mail
Peter (no plan)				X		X		quarterly
Helpful for most students	X	X	X	X	X	X		X

Note: Based on the needs of some of my students, I will make the following available for all students: check for understanding, graphic organizers per unit, daily agenda, reminder (posted and verbal) of homework assignments, electronic flashcard program for every unit.

Key: IEP = individualized education program; 504 = Section 504 plan

Figure 6.1. Accommodations matrix.

MAINTAINING CONFIDENTIALITY

As teams begin to discuss the information that is necessary to support the learning and growth of all students, every team member, including the paraprofessional, must have a firm understanding of the legal responsibility to keep student information confidential. Given the specialized instruction and ongoing interaction among students with disabilities, their families, and education team members, team members typically learn more information about these students and families than about students without disabilities and their families. This information is private and must not be shared beyond the family and the education team. Not only is discussing this information disrespectful, but according to IDEA 2004 it is potentially illegal (20 U.S.C. §1412[a][8]; §1417[c]). The education team is legally responsible for keeping this information confidential and private. As a member of a specific team, the paraprofessional may discuss information about a student or the student's family with other members when it is directly relevant to the student's education. Such discussions are to take place in a private location in the school (e.g., a classroom when students are not present or a meeting room) rather than a public location (e.g., faculty lounge, hallway). Every team member must remember that it is his or her responsibility to treat all students and adults with honor and respect. Suggested guidelines for confidentiality are listed in Table 6.3.

As a team, review your school's confidentiality policies and procedures. Issues of confidentiality are important enough to be discussed even for highly experienced team members. Refer to Para Form 25: Confidentiality Scenarios (located in the Para Forms appen-

Table 6.3. Guidelines for confidentiality

Things for paraprofessionals to avoid	Replacement suggestions for paraprofessionals
Never discuss information about a student in a public place (e.g., faculty lounge, hallway, grocery store).	Request that a meeting with the classroom teacher or special educator be in a private space (e.g., classroom).
Never discuss information about one student with the parents of another student.	Respond to such a request with "Respectfully, Mrs. Smith, it would be inappropriate for me to discuss another student or family with you," or "We have a fairly strict confidentiality policy to protect students and families. I think this would breach that policy; let me check with the teacher before I talk about this," or "I'm sorry, but I am not comfortable with this discussion; perhaps the teacher could assist you."
Never discuss information about one student with another student.	If students with and without disabilities are engaged in a cooperative activity, students may need to know specific information about one another to offer mutual support. In such situations, it is important for the team (including the student's parents and the student) to discuss what information is appropriate to share. For example, it may be helpful for a student without disabilities to know how to push his friend's wheelchair. It also might be important for a student with disabilities to know that his or her friend without disabilities gets upset easily.
Never discuss information about a student with school personnel who are not considered members of that student's service-providing team.	Ask yourself whether or not the person is on the student's team; if not, find the appropriate team member with whom you can discuss any issues about the student.
Do not access student records inappropriately.	Ask the teacher what type of information you need and how to obtain it. Ask him or her to explain the school policies on accessing records.
Do not create your own files on a student or family.	Only take data as directed by certified personnel, and then give the data to the person who requested it.
Never breach confidentiality.	Review the confidentiality policies of your specific school with your immediate supervisor at least annually. If you have questions about the policies and procedures regarding confidentiality in your school, speak to your supervisor immediately.

dix) for specific situations on confidentiality that would require a decision to be made. Read each situation and apply your school's policies to make a decision for each scenario. Every member's perspective adds to the richness of consideration in the decision-making process. In addition, Para Form 26: Addressing Confidentiality worksheet, located in the Para Forms appendix, presents a series of questions that all members of the team should address.

Reflection

Take a minute to think about the importance of confidentiality in your life. Are there areas of your own life that you entrust to friends or other professionals to keep confidential? How would you feel if that confidence was broken?

Write down and memorize a phrase you can use when you are in a situation that may be involve a breach of confidentiality. For example, you might say, "I'm not comfortable engaging actively or passively in conversations about a student's family outside of a team meeting" or "I think Ms. Jones, the special educator, would be a better source of information on that topic."

Paraprofessional Self-Advocacy

Ask the special educator to review the school's confidentiality policy with you. After listing the three to five most important elements, apply the policy to the scenarios that are included in this chapter.

ACTIVITY 12

A Situation You Know About

One member of the team describes a situation that requires confidentiality and a quick decision on the part of school personnel. Then each member of the team writes down how he or she should respond to the situation, keeping confidentiality policies in mind. Discuss this as a team. *Note:* An important dimension of this activity is to illustrate that everyone on the team is bound by the same confidentiality policies.

References

Baumgart, D., Brown, L., Pumpian, I., Nisbet, J., Ford, A., Sweet, M., et al. (1982). Principle of partial participation and individualized adaptations in education programs for severely handicapped students. *Journal of the Association for Persons with Severe Handicaps (JASH)*, 7, 17–27.

Broer, S.M., Doyle, M.B., & Giangreco, M.F. (2005). Perspectives of students with intellectual disabilities about their experiences with paraprofessional support. *Exceptional Children*, 71(4), 415–430.

Brown, F., Belz, P., Corsi, L., & Wenig, B. (1993). Choice diversity for people with severe disabilities. *Education and Training in Mental Retardation*, 28(6), 318–326.

Brown, F., Evans, I., Weed, K., & Owen, V. (1987). Delineating functional competencies: A component model. *Journal of the Association for Persons with Severe Handicaps*, 12(2), 117–124.

Campbell, C., Campbell, S., Collicott, J., Perner, D., & Stone, J. (1988). Individual instruction. *Education—New Brunswick Journal of Education*, 3, 17–20.

Causton-Theoharis, J., Giangreco, M.F., Doyle, M.B., & Vadasy, P. (2007). Paraprofessionals: The *sous chefs* of literacy instruction. *Teaching Exceptional Children*, 40(1), 56–62.

Causton-Theoharis, J.N., & Malgren, K.W. (2005). Building bridges: Strategies to help paraprofessionals promote peer interactions. *Teaching Exceptional Children*, 37(6), 18–24.

Code of Federal Regulations. (1999). 34SS 300.2.

Chopra, R.V., & French, N.K. (2004). Paraeducator relationships with parents of students with significant disabilities. *Remedial and Special Education*, 25(4), 240–251.

Devlin, P. (2005). Effects of continuous improvement training on student interaction and engagement. *Research and Practice for Persons with Severe Disabilities*, 30(2), 47–59.

Doyle, M.B. (2000). Connecting teachers and their students with disabilities through improved transition experiences. *Educational Leadership*, 58(1), 46–48.

Doyle, M.B. (2002). Paraprofessionals as members of the team: Supporting students with behavioral difficulties. In K.L. Lane, F.M. Gresham, & T.E. O'Shaughnessy (Eds.), *Interventions for children with or at-risk for emotional and behavioral disorders* (pp. 279–298). Boston: Allyn & Bacon.

Durand, V.M. (1988). Motivational Assessment Scale. In M. Hersen & A.S. Bellack (Eds.), *Dictionary of behavioral assessment techniques* (pp. 309–310). New York: Pergamon Press.

Evans, I.M., & Meyer, L.H. (1985). *An educative approach to behavior problems: A practical decision making model for interventions with severely handicapped learners*. Baltimore: Paul H. Brookes Publishing Co.

Ferguson, D.L. & Baumgart, D. (1991). Partial participation revisited. *Journal of the Association for Persons with Severe Handicaps (JASH)*, 16(4), 218–227.

French, N.K. (2001). Supervising paraprofessionals: A survey of teacher practices. *The Journal of Special Education*, 35, 41–53.

French, N.K., & Pickett, A.L. (1997). Paraprofessionals in special education: Issues for teacher educators. *Teacher Education and Special Education*, 20(1), 61–73.

Ghere, G., & York-Barr, J. (2007). Paraprofessional turnover and retention in inclusive programs: Hidden costs and promising practices. *Remedial and Special Education*, 28, 21–32.

Ghere, G., York-Barr, J., & Sommerness, J. (2002). *Supporting students with disabilities in inclusive schools: A curriculum for job-embedded paraprofessional development.* Minneapolis: University of Minnesota Institute on Community Education.

Giangreco, M.F. (1996). *Vermont interdependent services team approach (VISTA): A guide to coordinating educational services.* Baltimore: Paul H. Brookes Publishing Co.

Giangreco, M.F., Baumgart, D., & Doyle, M.B. (1995). Including students with learning disabilities in general education classrooms: How it can facilitate teaching and learning. *Intervention in School and Clinic, 30*(5), 273–278.

Giangreco, M.F., Broer, S.M., & Edelman, S.W. (1999). The tip of the iceberg: Determining whether paraprofessional support is needed for students with disabilities in general education settings. *Journal of the Association for Persons with Severe Handicaps, 24*(4), 281–291.

Giangreco, M.F., Broer, S.M., & Edelman, S.W. (2001). Teacher engagement with students with disabilities: Differences based on paraprofessional service delivery models. *Journal of the Association for Persons with Severe Handicaps, 26,* 75–86.

Giangreco, M.F., Broer, S.M., & Edelman, S.W. (2002). Schoolwide planning to improve paraeducator supports: A pilot study. *Rural Special Education Quarterly, 21*(1), 3–15.

Giangreco, M.F., Cloninger, C.J., & Iverson, V.S. (1998). *Choosing outcomes and accommodations for children (COACH): A guide to educational planning for students with disabilities (2nd ed.).* Baltimore: Paul H. Brookes Publishing Co.

Giangreco, M.F., Edelman, S.W., & Broer, S.M. (2003). Schoolwide planning to improve paraeducator supports. *Exceptional Children, 70*(1), 63–79.

Giangreco, M.F., Edelman, S., Broer, S., & Doyle, M.B. (2001). Paraprofessional support of students with disabilities: Literature from the past decade. *Exceptional Children, 68*(1), 45–64.

Giangreco, M.F., Edelman, S., Luiselli, T.E., & MacFarland, S.Z.C. (1997). Helping or hovering? Effects of instructional assistant proximity on students with disabilities. *Exceptional Children, 64,* 7–18.

Giangreco, M.F., Putnam, J. (1991). Supporting the education of students with severe disabilities in regular education environments. In L.H. Meyer, C. Peck, & L. Brown (Eds.), *Critical issues in the lives of people with severe disabilities* (pp. 245–270). Baltimore: Paul H. Brookes Publishing Co.

Giangreco, M.F, Suter, J.C., & Doyle, M.B. (in press). Recent research on paraprofessionals in inclusion-oriented schools. *Journal of Educational and Psychological Consultation.*

Green, J.E., & Barnes, D.L. (1989). *Do your aides aid instruction? A tool for assessing the use of paraprofessionals as instructional assistants.* Muncie, IN: Ball State University.

Hedeen, D., & Ayers, B. (1998, November). *Positive behavior support plan.* Paper presented at the meeting of The Association for Persons with Severe Handicaps, Seattle, WA.

Hunton, P., & Doyle, M.B. (1999, October). I'm not special ed. anymore: My name is Peter Hunton. *The Association for Persons with Severe Handicaps Newsletter, 25*(10), 22.

Individuals with Disabilities Education Act of 1990, PL 101-476, 20 U.S.C. §§ 1400 *et seq.*

Individuals with Disabilities Education Act Amendments of 1997, PL 105-17, 20 U.S.C. §§ 1400 *et seq.*

Individuals with Disabilities Education Improvement Act of 2004, PL 108-446, 20 U.S.C. §§ 1400 *et seq.*

Logue, O.J. (1993, April). *Job satisfaction and retention variables of special education paraeducators.* Paper presented at the twelfth annual conference on the Training and Employment of the Paraprofessional Workforce in Education, Rehabilitation, and Related Fields, Seattle.

No Child Left Behind Act of 2001, PL 107-110, 115 Stat. 1425, 20 U.S.C. §§ 6301 *et seq.*

Pickett, A.L., Litkins, M., & Wallace, T. (2003). *The employment and preparation of paraeducators.* New York: National Resource Center for Paraprofessionals in Education Related Services.

Quilty, K.M. (2007). Teaching paraprofessionals how to write and implement social stories for students with autism spectrum disorders. *Remedial and Special Education, 28,* 182–189.

Rainforth, B., & York-Barr, J. (1997). *Collaborative teams for students with severe disabilities: Integrating therapy and educational services* (2nd ed). Baltimore: Paul H. Brookes Publishing Co.

Riggs, C.G. (2004, May/June). To teachers: What paraeducators want you to know. *Teaching Exceptional Children, 36*(5), 8–12.

Riggs, C.G., & Mueller, P.H. (2001). Employment and utilization of paraeducators in inclusive settings. *Journal of Special Education 35,* 54–62.

Selected paraeducator references. (n.d.). Retrieved July 12, 2007, from http://www.uvm.edu/~cdci/?Page=parasupport/chrono.html

Snyder, T.D., Tan, A.G., & Hoffman, C.M. (2006). *Digest of education statistics 2005* (NCES 2006-030). Washington, DC: U.S. Government Printing Office.

Thompson, J.R., Meadan, H., Fansler, K.W., Alber, S.B., & Balogh, P.A. (2007, July/August). Family assessment portfolios: A new way to jumpstart family/school collaboration. *Teaching Exceptional Children, 39*(6) 19–25.

Udvari-Solner, A. (1992). *Curricular adaptations: Accommodating the instructional needs of diverse learners.* Topeka: Kansas State Board of Education.

U.S. Department of Education. (1993). *Twelfth annual report to Congress on the implementation of the Handicapped Children's Education Act.* Washington, DC: Author.

U.S. Department of Education. (2002). *Title I paraprofessionals: Non-regulatory guidance.* Retrieved July 6, 2007, from http//www.ed.gov/policu/elsec/guid/paraguidance.pdf

U.S. Department of Education. (2007). *Annual report tables: IDEA Part B Personnel.* Retrieved June 1, 2007, from http://www.ideadata.org/PartBReport.asp

U.S. Department of Education, Office of Special Education Programs Data Analysis System. (2000). *Twenty-second annual report to Congress on the implementation of the Individuals with Disabilities Education Act.* Washington, DC: U.S. Government Printing Office.

Vaughn, S., Bos, C.S., & Schumm, J.S. (2003). *Teaching exceptional, diverse, and at-risk students in the general education classroom* (3rd ed.) Boston: Allyn & Bacon.

Werts, M.G., Harris, S., Tillery, C.Y., & Roark, R. (2004). What parents tell us about paraeducators. *Remedial and Special Education, 25*, 232–239.

York-Barr, J., Doyle, M.B., & Kronberg, R. M. (1996). *Creative inclusive school communities: A staff development series for general and special educators.* Baltimore: Paul H. Brookes Publishing Co.

Resources

Center for Multilingual and Multicultural Research
http://www.uvm.edu/~cdci/parasupport

The Minnesota Paraprofessional Consortium
http://ici2.umn.edu/para

National Clearinghouse for Paraeducator Resources: Paraeducator Pathways into Teaching
http://www.usc.edu/dept/education/CMMR/Clearinghouse.html

The National Early Childhood Technical Assistance Center
http://www.nectac.org/topics/personnel/paraprof.asp

National Joint Committee on Learning Disabilities
http://www.idonline.org/about/partners/njcld

National Resource Center for Paraprofessionals
http://www.nrcpara.org

Paraeducator Training Resources
http://para2.unl.edu/ec

The PAR2A Center
http://www.paracenter.org/PARACenter

TRISPED: Staff Training Solutions
http://www.trisped.org

A

Activities

Activity 1a   Create-a-Paraprofessional

Activity 1b   Create-a-General Educator

Activity 1c   Create-a-Special Educator

Activity 2   Activity Debriefing

Activity 3   Role Clarification with a Twist

Activity 5*   The Paraprofessional's Daily Schedule

Activity 6   Discussion About the Paraprofessional's Daily Schedule

Activity 10   Creating a Positive Atmosphere

Note: Activities 4, 7, 8, and 9 do not have corresponding forms.

Create-a-Paraprofessional

As a team, draw the ideal paraprofessional. Be prepared to share your creation with the whole group!

Discussion: What does your team do to support the paraprofessional in moving closer to becoming the "ideal" paraprofessional? How does your team provide the paraprofessional with information, training, and feedback? How might this improve?

Create-a-General Educator

As a team, draw the ideal general educator. Be prepared to share your creation with the whole group!

Discussion: What does your team do to support the general educator in moving closer to becoming the "ideal" general educator? How does your team provide the general educator with information, training, and feedback? How might this improve?

Create-a-Special Educator

As a team, draw the ideal special educator. Be prepared to share your creation with the whole group!

Discussion: What does your team do to support the special educator in moving closer to becoming the "ideal" special educator? How does your team provide the special educator with information, training, and feedback? How might this improve?

Activity Debriefing

As a team, reflect on each of the creations. Discuss the following questions:

What are the similarities and differences among the creations? Remember, if there are too many similarities, there is a lack of understanding of the appropriate roles and responsibilities.

_____

_____

_____

_____

_____

_____

What do you understand better as a result of having participated in this introductory activity?

_____

_____

_____

_____

_____

What are the implications for training and support for the paraprofessional as well as other team members?

_____

_____

_____

_____

_____

_____

Role Clarification with a Twist
(Transparency Master)

The Paraprofessional's Daily Schedule

Directions: The general educator, the special educator, and the paraprofessional need to work together to develop the paraprofessional's daily schedule. This schedule should reflect the paraprofessional's duties that are related to supporting the general learning environment as well as individual students. After the schedule has been drafted, use Activity 6: Discussion About the Paraprofessional's Daily Schedule to determine whether the schedule needs revision.

Time	Typical class or activity	Paraprofessional's typical responsibilities

Discussion About the Paraprofessional's Daily Schedule

Directions: After the paraprofessionals' daily schedule has been developed, the classroom teacher, the special educator, and the paraprofessional should meet to discuss the question listed on this worksheet. The answer to the question may necessitate an immediate revision of the paraprofessional's daily schedule or a revision in the future.

In reviewing the paraprofessional's daily schedule, to what extent is he or she engaged in activities related only to the student with disabilities?

None of the time		Some of the time		All of the time	
0	1	2	3	4	5

As a team, discuss whether the level of interaction that the paraprofessional has with the student who has a disability is appropriate. Keep in mind that when adults (e.g., paraprofessional, general educator, special educator) remain in close proximity to a student with disabilities, classmates are less likely to approach and interact with the student. As a team, you may discover that is necessary to develop a formal plan to support the student with disabilities in becoming less dependent on the paraprofessional or other adult team members.

Creating a Positive Atmosphere

Actions that contribute positive energy	Actions that contribute negative energy
Students with disabilities sit among their peer group at lunch and in the classroom.	Students with disabilities sit with adults and are physically separate from their peers.
Classroom teacher interacts with and teaches the student with disabilities.	Paraprofessional delivers instruction to the student with disabilities. The special educator delivers instruction in a separate class.
Paraprofessional provides support and assistance to all students in the classroom under the direction of the teacher.	Paraprofessional provides support exclusively to the student with disabilities.
Teachers and paraprofessionals greet each student as he or she enters the classroom.	Paraprofessional interacts exclusively with the student with disabilities. The teacher does not greet or acknowledge the student.
Adults always speak with students in kind and respectful ways, never yelling or being unkind.	Adults raise their voices and yell at students.
Adults confer and plan with individual students to improve their behaviors.	Adults use humiliation, power, and control to change behaviors.
Your idea #1:	
Your idea #2:	
Your idea #3:	

B

Para Forms

Para Form 1   Community Self-Assessment Checklist

Para Form 2   The Paraprofessional's Responsibilities

Para Form 3   Advocacy Skills for Paraprofessionals: Asking for What You Need

Para Form 4   Welcome Interview

Para Form 5   Classroom Routine

Para Form 6   Up-Front Issues to Reach Consensus On

Para Form 7   Problem-Solving on the Fly

Para Form 8   Student Profile

Para Form 9   Participation in Daily Classroom Routines

Para Form 10   Individualized Education Program Matrix

Para Form 11   Student Learning Priorities and Support

Para Form 12   Effective Utilization of Paraprofessional Support

Para Form 13   Common Components of Daily Routines: Practice with a Familiar Routine

Para Form 14   Common Components of Daily Routines: Apply to a Student's Schedule

Para Form 15   Common Components of Daily Routines: Planning Worksheet

Para Form 16   Discussion of Prompting Strategies

Para Form 17   Instructional Support Plan

Para Form 18   Communicative Intent of Adult Behaviors

Para Form 19   Schedule Analysis

Para Form 20   Determining Communicative Intent via Antecedent–Behavior–Consequence

Para Form 21   Responsibilities Related to Encouraging Positive Classroom Behaviors

Para Form 22   Team Communication

Para Form 23   Meeting Agenda

Para Form 24   Documenting Spontaneous Incidents

Para Form 25   Confidentiality Scenarios

Para Form 26   Addressing Confidentiality

Community Self-Assessment Checklist

Action	Student with disabilities	What would it take to make this happen?
Rides the regular bus		
Enters the school through the common door		
Has locker and desk among classmates		
Transitions with classmates		
Initiates interactions with classmates		
Sits with classmates at lunch, recess, and so on		
Works in groups with classmates		
Classmates initiate interactions		

Action	Teacher	Para-professional	What would it take to make this happen?
(Teacher) Addresses students directly in casual conversations as well as during instruction			
(Teacher) Incorporates learning styles, strengths, and needs into instruction			
Is familiar with school and classroom policies (e.g., fire drills, classroom routine, contact with families) and procedures			
Knows explicitly stated roles and responsibilities			
Has written daily schedule			
Has written instructional plans			
Receives initial and ongoing staff development			

The Paraprofessional's Responsibilities

Directions: As a team, rank the paraprofessional's responsibilities, and check the items that require training.

Noninstructional responsibility	Training	Priority	Instructional responsibility	Training	Priority
Perform clerical and organizational tasks (e.g., attendance, lunch count)			Assist with classroom management by implementing classroom rules		
Monitor students in the hallway, on the playground, and at the bus stop			Implement teacher-designed instruction with individual students, small groups, and large		
Supervise students during meals and snacks			Tutor individual students		
Operate audiovisual equipment in the classroom			Contribute ideas and suggestions related to instruction		
Provide specific personal care for students (e.g., restroom use, repositioning)			Participate in team meetings		
Additional task:			Additional task:		
Additional task:			Additional task:		
Additional task:			Additional task:		
Additional task:			Additional task:		

Advocacy Skills for Paraprofessionals
Asking for What You Need

Directions: As a paraprofessional, you are likely to receive at least some on-the-job training. It may prove helpful to think about what it is that you need to learn in order to provide appropriate assistance. Using clarifying statements and questions will increase the likelihood that you are provided with the support that you need and that you take responsibility for your own professional development.

The special educator or general educator provides the paraprofessional with instructional information for one or more students. The information must include the:

- Instructional goal
- Instructional strategy
- Identification of the evidence

The paraprofessional reads the information and says:

A. It is my understanding that the instructional outcome is _____.
    The instructional strategy is _____.
    The evidence will be _____.

    Is this accurate?
    ☐ YES   ☐ NO

B. Will you demonstrate the instructional strategy for me?
    ☐ YES   ☐ NO

    When can you do this?
    Date: _____   Time: _____

    Will you model the strategy in the same context that I will be using it (e.g., general education classroom, library)?
    ☐ YES   ☐ NO

    Will you observe and give me feedback using the strategy in context?
    ☐ YES   ☐ NO

    When can you do this?
    Date: _____   Time: _____

Welcome Interview

	Paraprofessional	General educator	Special educator	Extended team member
1. What made you decide to work with children and youth in a school environment?				
2. What do you hope students will learn from you?				
3. What do you think contributes to making a classroom a positive learning environment?				
4. Who is the paraprofessional's supervisor? What are his or her responsibilities?				

(continued)

	Paraprofessional	General educator	Special educator	Extended team member
5. Take a few minutes to clarify the *paraprofessional's* responsibilities. Focus on general areas related to classroom function rather than student-specific responsibilities.				
6. Take a few minutes to clarify the *general educator's* responsibilities.				
7. Take a few minutes to clarify the *special educator's* responsibilities.				
8. What do you need to do your job well? How can team members support you?				

	Paraprofessional	General educator	Special educator	Extended team member
9. Who is responsible for showing the paraprofessional how to support students with and without disabilities?				
10. Are there specific issues, questions, or concerns that you feel need to be addressed during the next several days or weeks?				
11. If you could fast-forward to the end of the school year, what would you hope to have experienced, learned, and accomplished? For your team? For your students? For yourself?				

Classroom Routine

Directions: In the first and second column, enter the time and activity. In the third column, enter the typical tasks associated with each activity. In the fourth and fifth columns, check who will complete the tasks: the teacher, the paraprofessional, or both. As a team, discuss this routine.

Time	Activity	Tasks	Teacher	Paraprofessional	Comments

Up-Front Issues to Reach Consensus On

Directions: As a team, discuss and answer each of the following questions prior to the first day of school.

Planning

1. How will the paraprofessional participate in planning instruction for students with and without disabilities?

    _____ Directly sharing ideas during weekly meetings
    _____ Indirectly through informal conversations during the week
    _____ Not at all

2. When and where will these meetings occur?

    _____ Day   _____ Time   _____ Location

Instruction

3. Will the paraprofessional help implement instruction?

    _____ Student with disabilities   _____ Students without disabilities

4. How will the paraprofessional help implement instruction?

    _____ Facilitation of teacher-designed instruction
    _____ One-to-one   _____ Small groups   _____ Whole class
    _____ Implementation of teacher-designed adaptations
    _____ Not at all
    _____ Other

5. Who will train the paraprofessional to use the specific instruction strategies?

    _____ General educator   _____ Special educator

    When will this training occur?

    _____ Daily   _____ Weekly   _____ Monthly

6. Who will evaluate the effectiveness of the instruction?

    _____ General educator   _____ Special educator

Student Behavior

7. What are the classroom expectations (i.e., classroom rules) for student and adults?

8. How are classroom expectations communicated to the students?

9. What is the plan to address unacceptable student behaviors in a timely manner?

10. What are the specific roles of the general educator, special educator, and paraprofessional in supporting positive student behaviors?

_____

(continued)

Communication

11. How will we address our communication needs with each other?

12. Who will communicate with parents about

     Routine daily occurrences?

     _____ General educator   _____ Special educator   _____ Paraprofessional

     Unusual situations?

     _____ General educator   _____ Special educator

Evaluation

13. How are most students evaluated?

     _____ Portfolios
     _____ Weekly tests
     _____ Performances
     _____ Other:

14. Who is responsible for the evaluations?

     _____ General educator   _____ Special educator

15. How is this the same or different for the student with the disabilities?

16. Will the student be receiving a report card?

     _____ Yes   _____ No

17. If the student with disabilities will receive a report card, who will adapt the report card and monitor the student's progress?

     _____ General educator   _____ Special educator

     When will the evaluation occur?

     What types of evidence are necessary to the evaluation?

Next Meeting

Date:
Time:
Location:
Topics to address:

Notes:

Problem-Solving on the Fly

Directions: Keep several copies of this form in a three-ring notebook that team members have access to throughout the week. As issues arise, jot them down and formally address them during the team meeting.

Date:

Problem to be solved:

Relevant Information:

Suggestions to remedy the problem:

Discussion:

Solution:

People responsible:

Student Profile

Student: _____   Paraprofessional: _____

Parents: _____   General educator: _____

Friends: _____   Special educator: _____

About the Student

1. What are this student's strengths?

2. Over the past 6 months, in what areas has the student shown the most growth?

3. What is the student's learning style? (circle one)

Visual-linguistic	Auditory	Body-kinesthetic
Musical-rhythmic	Interpersonal	Other

4. How does the student communicate? (circle as many as apply)

Verbal	Gestural	Cued speech
Sign language	Hand gestures	Letter or word board
Facilitated communication	Objects	Head movements
Objects	Pictures	Eye gaze
Facial expressions	Picture symbols	Other:

5. Does the student need assistance with communication?   ❏ No   ❏ Yes

   Please describe:

6. How do peers assist this student with communication?

Classroom Information

7. Describe the student's literacy skills or level.

   a. Picture reading:

   b. Sight word recognition:

   c. Fluency:

   d. Comprehension:

   e. Favorite books:

_____

(continued)

8. How does the student access written information?

    a. Same text as peers

    b. Multilevel curriculum at the _____ reading level

    c. Books on tape

    d. Other:

9. What types of technology has the student used in the past?

Remote control devices	Switches	Computer games (names)
PowerPoint	Internet searching	Inspiration
Kidspiration	Other software:	Other hardware:

Peer Relationships

10. Who are the student's friends?

    a. What do they do during school together? Is this frequently prompted by an adult?

    b. What do they do after school or on weekends? Is this frequently prompted by an adult?

Teaching Information

11. What do you do to leverage the student's strengths?

12. How do you facilitate the student's connection with peers?

13. How do you facilitate a sense of belonging and contribution on behalf of the student with disabilities?

14. In the past, what specific instructional strategies have and have not been successful?

15. If a paraprofessional will be involved in supporting this student, what are the expectations for him or her?

Summary

Based on this conversation, what areas need to be addressed this year?

Participation in Daily Classroom Routines

Directions: Check the appropriate box for each question. One sun means the student is just learning and may need some help. Two suns mean that he or she is getting pretty good but might need a little help. Three suns mean, "Watch out! I can do this myself!"

Student: _____ Special educator: _____

General educator: _____ Paraprofessional: _____

Classroom participation skills	☀	☀☀	☀☀☀
1. Listens and looks at the speaker One-to-one Small group Large group			
2. Requests help			
3. Says "please" and "thank you"			
4. Brings materials to class			
5. Follows _____-step verbal directions Follows _____-step written directions			
6. Completes in-school assignments			
7. Contributes to conversations One-to-one with a peer One-to-one with an adult Small group with peers Small group with adults Large group with peers Large group with adults			
8. Asks questions			
9. Ignores common classroom distractions			
10. Decides on something to do when Presented with a choice Presented with a situation			

(continued)

Relationship skills	☀	☀☀	☀☀☀

11. Introduces him- or herself
     To peers
     To adults			

12. Initiates conversation
     With peers
     With adults			

13. Ends conversation
     With peers
     With adults			

14. Plays a game
     With peers
     With adults			

15. Offers assistance
     To peers
     To adults			

16. Gives compliments
     To peers
     To adults			

17. Suggests an activity to do
     With peers
     With adults			

18. Shares toys and materials
     With peers
     With adults			

19. Apologizes
     To peers
     To adults			

20. Other			

Individualized Education Program Matrix

Directions: List the student's daily activities or class periods across the top row. Then list a student's learning priorities in the left-hand column. Place a check in each of the corresponding boxes in which each learning priority will be addressed throughout the school day.

Student: _____   Grade: _____

General educator: _____

Special educator: _____

Paraprofessional: _____

	Daily activities/Class periods							
Individualized education program goals								

Student Learning Priorities and Support

Directions: In the left-hand column, check whether you will use a multilevel approach or a curriculum overlapping approach. Then, list the student's learning priorities that need to be addressed during the day and in a specific class. In the center and right-hand columns, list the instructional strategy and check the supports (people and/or materials) that are necessary for the student to accomplish his or her learning priorities.

Student: _____

General educator: _____

Special educator: _____

Paraprofessional: _____

Learning priorities (What)	Instructional strategy (How)	Support (People and/or materials)
Learning priorities for the day ❏ Curriculum overlapping ❏ Multilevel instruction		*People:* ❏ Friends ❏ Classroom teacher ❏ Special educator ❏ Paraprofessional *Materials:*
Learning priorities for _____ class ❏ Curriculum overlapping ❏ Multilevel instruction		*People:* ❏ Friends ❏ Classroom teacher ❏ Special educator ❏ Paraprofessional *Materials:*
Learning priorities for _____ class ❏ Curriculum overlapping ❏ Multilevel instruction		*People:* ❏ Friends ❏ Classroom teacher ❏ Special educator ❏ Paraprofessional *Materials:*

Effective Utilization of Paraprofessional Support

Directions: Apply the series of statements in the left column to a specific class period during the day.

Student: _____

General educator: _____

Special educator: _____

Paraprofessional: _____

Area of support	Describe how and when this area is working well.	Describe how and when this area needs change.
The paraprofessional provides supplementary instruction, not primary instruction.		
Instruction is designed in a manner that does not require significant decision making by the paraprofessional.		
Proven instructional methods are used.		
The paraprofessional is trained in the instructional approach and/or program he or she implements.		
The paraprofessional is monitored.		

Common Components of Daily Routines
Practice with a Familiar Routine

Directions: Apply the common components framework to a typical activity or routine that you engage in every day.

Student: _____

Routine or activity: _____

	Your participation
Initiate How do you know it is time to begin this activity (e.g., alarm rings, refer to your personal schedule)?	
Prepare What do you need to do in order to be ready for the activity (e.g., gather certain materials)?	
Core What do you actually *do?* How do you participate?	
Terminate How do you know when the activity is over?	
As part of this routine, which interwoven components will be targeted for instruction or support (e.g., communication, interaction with others, choice making, problem solving)?	

From Brown, F., Evans, I., Weed, K., & Owen, V. (1987). Delineating functional competencies: A component model. *Journal of the Association for Persons with Severe Handicaps, 12*(2), 199; adapted by permission.

Common Components of Daily Routines
Apply to a Student's Schedule

Directions: As a team, apply the common components framework to an activity or routine that a student engages in daily. First, consider how the student does or could participate in each component. Then, consider how to support the student in participating in each component.

Student: _____

Routine or activity: _____

	Student participation What will the student do? Where will the student be?	**Support** What will you do? Where will you be?
Initiate How do you know it is time to begin this activity (e.g., alarm rings, refer to your personal schedule)?		
Prepare What do you need to do order to be ready for the activity (e.g., gather certain materials)?		
Core What do you actually *do?* How do you participate?		
Terminate How do you know when the activity is over?		

As part of this routine, which interwoven components will be targeted for instruction or support (e.g., communication, interaction with others, choice making, problem solving)?

From Brown, F., Evan, I., Weed, K., & Owen, V. (1987). Delineating functional competencies: A component model. *Journal of The Association for Persons with Severe Handicaps, 12*(2), 19; adapted by permission.

Common Components of Daily Routines
Planning Worksheet

Directions: Use this form with Para Form 14: Common Components of Daily Routines: Apply to a Student's Schedule to describe which interwoven components will be targeted for each major daily routine.

Student: _____

Routine or activity: _____

	Student participation What will the student do? Where will the student be?	Support What will you do? Where will you be?
Communication		
Interacting with others		
Choice making		
Problem solving		
Monitoring quality		
Monitoring tempo		
Movement and positioning		

Discussion of Prompting Strategies

Directions: The purpose of this worksheet is to guide your team in discussing a variety of instructional prompts. List four of the student's learning priorities (from the student's IEP) in the first column. Then, as a team, discuss and identify the type of prompts that are likely to assist this student in accomplishing each learning priority. Finally, discuss and identify the people who might provide this assistance.

Student: _____

Learning priorities	Types of prompts	Who might provide this assistance?
	____ Natural ____ Gestural ____ Indirect verbal ____ Direct verbal ____ Model ____ Partial physical ____ Full physical	____ Classmates ____ Adults
	____ Natural ____ Gestural ____ Indirect verbal ____ Direct verbal ____ Model ____ Partial physical ____ Full physical	____ Classmates ____ Adults
	____ Natural ____ Gestural ____ Indirect verbal ____ Direct verbal ____ Model ____ Partial physical ____ Full physical	____ Classmates ____ Adults
	____ Natural ____ Gestural ____ Indirect verbal ____ Direct verbal ____ Model ____ Partial physical ____ Full physical	____ Classmates ____ Adults

Instructional Support Plan

Directions: Team members can use this form to document student learning priorities, appropriate prompts, and adaptations. For the last column, you can list both ongoing adaptations and preplanned, unit-specific adaptations.

Student: _____

General educator: _____

Special educator: _____

Paraprofessional: _____

Activity	Learning priorities	Instructional prompts		Suggested adaptations
1	For the whole class: For the student:	____ Natural ____ Gestural ____ Indirect verbal ____ Direct verbal ____ Model ____ Partial physical ____ Full physical	____ Peer ____ General educator ____ Special educator ____ Paraprofessional ____ Related service personnel	Ongoing adaptation: Unit-specific accommodation:
2	For the whole class: For the student:	____ Natural ____ Gestural ____ Indirect verbal ____ Direct verbal ____ Model ____ Partial physical ____ Full physical	____ Peer ____ General educator ____ Special educator ____ Paraprofessional ____ Related service personnel	Ongoing adaptation: Unit-specific accommodation:
3	For the whole class: For the student:	____ Natural ____ Gestural ____ Indirect verbal ____ Direct verbal ____ Model ____ Partial physical ____ Full physical	____ Peer ____ General educator ____ Special educator ____ Paraprofessional ____ Related service personnel	Ongoing adaptation: Unit-specific accommodation:

Communicative Intent of Adult Behaviors

Directions: This form provides a structure for adults to examine the potential impact of their own behaviors on student responses.

Adult behavior	Unintended impact	Alternative adult response
Yelling at students to get their attention	Loss of control Power assertion Intimidation Inability to figure out what to do	Use visual or auditory cue to attract attention (e.g., lights, small bell, *3-2-1 look at me*) Ask for a minute to collect self Deliberately speak in a soft voice
Posting students' names on the board for misbehavior	Humiliation Highlighting and adding to expected inappropriate responses from specific students	Converse one to one with the student to try to understand his or her behavior Use a solution-oriented approach Give differentiated assignments Develop expectations that are doable and therefore likely to create a new pattern of positive behaviors

Your turn: What adult behaviors does your team see or hear that have not been effective?

1. _____

2. _____

3. _____

4. _____

5. _____

6. _____

7. _____

8. _____

9. _____

Schedule Analysis

Directions: When a student displays an unusual, disruptive, or challenging behavior, fill in the time and activity. Then, circle the instructional format, the people present, and the teaching style. Next, complete the antecedent–behavior–consequence (A-B-C) fields. Using the communicative intent fields, try to determine what the student is trying to communicate and what the potential solutions will be.

Student: _____ General educator: _____

Special educator: _____ Paraprofessional: _____

Instructional format: Individual

Small group

Large group

People present: Peers: _____

General educator   Special educator   Paraprofessional

Teaching style: Lecture   Class discussion   Activity

Among students   Technology   Other: _____

Time	Activity	A	B	C	Communicative intent	Potential solutions
					☐ Attention seeking ☐ Escape/avoidance ☐ Getting something tangible ☐ Frustration with task ☐ Frustration with people ☐ Boredom	
					☐ Attention seeking ☐ Escape/avoidance ☐ Getting something tangible ☐ Frustration with task ☐ Frustration with people ☐ Boredom	
					☐ Attention seeking ☐ Escape/avoidance ☐ Getting something tangible ☐ Frustration with task ☐ Frustration with people ☐ Boredom	

Determining Communicative Intent via Antecedent–Behavior–Consequence

Antecedent What happened immediately before the difficult behavior occurred?	Behavior Describe what you heard and saw.	Consequence What happened immediately after the behavior?

Communicative intent:

❏ Attention seeking

❏ Escape or avoidance

❏ Obtaining something tangible

❏ Self-regulation

❏ Play

Interpretation:

Responsibilities Related to Encouraging Positive Classroom Behaviors

Responsibilities	General or special educator	Paraprofessional
Establish class routines, expectations, and/or rules.	X	
Schedule class activities and daily/weekly schedule.	X	
Establish behavioral goals for individuals or groups of students.	X	
Write the positive behavior support plan, including target behavior to increase (replacement behavior), target behavior to decrease, instructional plan to teach the replacement behavior, reinforcement and reinforcement schedule, consequences for/responses to not demonstrating appropriate behavior, data collection system, and review of data.	X	
Train the paraprofessional to implement the positive behavior support plan.	X	
Observe and provide feedback on the paraprofessional's implementation.	X	
Implement general classroom routines, expectations, and/or rules.	X	X
Implement individual behavior support plans.	X	X
Collect appropriate data.	X	X
Evaluate the effectiveness of classroom routines, expectations, and/or rules.	X	
Evaluate the effectiveness of individual positive behavior support plans.	X	
Use evaluation data to alter plans.	X	

Team Communication

Directions: As a team, discuss and identify when you will meet at least 30 minutes biweekly to discuss and plan for upcoming curriculum and instruction. During the planning session, clarify each team member's roles and responsibilities in relation to supporting all students.

1. Schedule meetings. Select one or more days for your team and identify specific times:

   ❏ Monday _____

   ❏ Tuesday _____

   ❏ Wednesday _____

   ❏ Thursday _____

   ❏ Friday _____

2. Topics to be addressed (check as many as apply):

   ❏ Curriculum

   ❏ Adaptations

   ❏ Teaching strategies

   ❏ Support strategies

   ❏ Other: _____

3. Team members expected to participate (check as many as apply):

   ❏ General educator

   ❏ Paraprofessional

   ❏ Special educator

   ❏ Extended team member: _____

   ❏ Extended team member: _____

4. List any exceptions or additions to these general plans (e.g., teacher in-service days, holidays, birthdays):

Meeting Agenda

Directions: This form may be used during team meetings when discussing the agenda, recording meeting minutes, or documenting outcomes.

1. Team members needed for this meeting:

   ❏ General educator
   ❏ Paraprofessional
   ❏ Special educator
   ❏ Extended team member:
   ❏ Extended team member:
   ❏ Parent/guardian
   ❏ Student

2. Members present at this meeting:

   ❏ General educator
   ❏ Paraprofessional
   ❏ Special educator
   ❏ Extended team member: _____
   ❏ Extended team member: _____

3. Topics to be addressed (check as many as apply):

   ❏ Curriculum
   ❏ Adaptations
   ❏ Teaching strategies
   ❏ Support strategies
   ❏ Other: _____

4. Given the upcoming unit activities, what needs to be developed and by whom?

5. Areas identified for training and the people responsible:

6. Next meeting:
   Date:_____
   Time:_____
   Location: _____
   Facilitator:_____
   Recorder:_____

Documenting Spontaneous Incidents

Directions: This worksheet is to be used by the paraprofessional for documenting challenging situations that occur during the day or week when there is not an immediate opportunity to problem-solve with the general or special educator. The paraprofessional should bring this form completed to team meetings so that the team can discuss how he or she handled the situation and, in some cases, proactively plan the most appropriate action if similar situations arise in the future.

Student: _____

Paraprofessional: _____

General educator: _____

Special educator: _____

Date of the incident: _____

1. Describe the situation from a "before, during, and after" perspective.

   Before: What do you remember happening to the student or in the environment immediately before the incident occurred?

   During: What did the student say or do?

   After: What happened immediately following the incident? How did you respond?

2. What was the outcome of the situation? Please be specific.

3. Did this incident bring to mind any specific area of training that you would like to receive?

4. Did this situation make you think that your team needs to agree on a proactive plan to avoid a recurrence?

Confidentiality Scenarios

Several situations related to confidentiality that require a decision to be made are presented in this form. Read each of the situations and apply your school's policies to make a decision for each scenario. Then discuss your response with other team members.

Student to Student

Avery is in a second-grade inclusive elementary classroom. He has moderate intellectual disabilities, and his speech is difficult to understand. During literacy block, students are working in groups of three. The teacher is working with one group at a time while the paraprofessional, Mr. Jackson, monitors the rest of the students, providing assistance when needed. Using language that is developmentally appropriate, Mr. Jackson approaches Avery's group and begins to tell the students without disabilities Avery's instructional goals for reading. The children seem pleased to know Avery's goals and are intent on helping him reach those goals in their small group. Mr. Jackson does not mention the goals of any other group member.

Discussion: Has the paraprofessional broken any rules about confidentiality? If so, which ones? What could he have done differently?

Key Points:

- The initial decision to share Avery's instructional goals should have been made by the team, including Avery's parents.
- If Avery's goals are being publicly identified, so should the goals of the other students in the group. For example, the paraprofessional could have said, "What is each person in the group working on?" or "What is your role in the cooperative group?"
- Team members, including the paraprofessional, must take care that Avery's life is not open for public discussion in a manner different from his peers.

Notes on your school's confidentiality policy:

(continued)

Hallway Conversation

Mrs. Franks is a well-respected paraprofessional at the middle school. She works with the seventh-grade team to support a variety of students with and without disabilities. As she is walking down the hallway, she overhears a conversation about a specific student and his family. The hushed tones of the conversation make Mrs. Franks uncomfortable. Before she knows it, one person involved in the conversation asks Mrs. Franks if the information is true about the student and his family.

Discussion: How should Mrs. Franks respond?

Key Points:

- The hallway is never considered a private place for a conversation.
- Would it be okay for the conversation to be taking place if the student and his family were present?
- What is the educational relevance of the information?

Notes on your school's confidentiality policy:

Generate a scenario that is relevant to your school situation. Identify the key points to the situation and how it should be resolved.

Community Helpers Example

Dolores is a paraprofessional who supports several students who have challenging behavior at the local school. She has been a paraprofessional for many years. Dolores is widely known in her community for her volunteer work at the local youth center. One of the students who Dolores supports attends the youth center regularly. One afternoon at the youth center, Dolores notices that the student is beginning to have some difficulty managing some of his behaviors. Dolores has learned several behavioral management techniques to support this student in school.

Discussion: What should Dolores do? Should she intervene at the youth center with the behavioral management techniques that she learned at school?

Key Points:

- Dolores is not working as a paraprofessional with the student at the youth center.
- Dolores is not a case manager.
- Dolores has learned specific and positive approaches to support the student.

Notes on your school's confidentiality policy:

Addressing Confidentiality

Directions: As a team, discuss the policies and procedures related to confidentiality as they apply to both students with and without disabilities, as well as their families.

1. How is confidentiality defined in our school policies?

2. What are the policies and procedures in this school related to confidentiality?

3. What are the expectations of the members of our team regarding confidentiality? How can our team support one another in maintaining respectful interactions and confidentiality in relation to he students and their families with whom we work?

4. How will we ensure that confidentiality is maintained in our daily work with students and their families?

5. What do we do when we are in situations in which we believe confidentiality is being breached? What are some phrases that we might use to discreetly remind another person of this issue?

Index

Tables, figures, and footnotes are indicated by *t*, *f*, and *n*, respectively.

A-B-C, *see* Antecedent–behavior–consequence

Accommodations, 67*t*, 68, 81–83, 116*t*
   see also Adaptations

Activities
   Activity 1 (Basic Role Differentiation), 10–13
   Activity 2 (Activity Debriefing), 12, 14
   Activity 3 (Role Clarification with a Twist), 14–15
   Activity 4 (What Is a Team?), 20–21
   Activity 5 (Developing the Paraprofessional's Daily
      Schedule), 24–25
   Activity 6 (Discussion About the Paraprofessional's
      Daily Schedule), 27*t*
   Activity 7 (Who Is Peter?), 49–50
   Activity 8 (Categorizing Goals and Objectives), 66–67
   Activity 9 (Positive Statements About Kids), 89
   Activity 10 (Creating a Positive Atmosphere), 90
   Activity 11 (Attention Seeking), 94–95
   Activity 12 (A Situation You Know About), 118
   see also Reflection activities

Adaptations, 63, 79–80

Adults
   effect on classroom atmosphere, 88, 89–90
   importance of modeling, 5, 77
   personal views of, 54–55
   see also Paraprofessionals; Teachers; Team

Advocacy Skills for Paraprofessionals: Asking for What
      You Need, *see* Para Form 3

Antecedent–behavior–consequence (A-B-C), 96, 97, 100,
101*t*

Assessment, 9, 30–31

Atmosphere, 89, 104–105

Attention Seeking, *see* Activity 11

Basic Role Differentiation, *see* Activity 1

Behavior
   challenging, 97–98
   designing a support plan for, 101–102, 102*f*, 103*f*
   finding the positive of each child, 89
   identifying communicative intent, 100–101
   implementing a behavior support plan, 104–109
   nonintrusive strategies for, 106*t*
   planned ignoring, 107–108
   positive, 106
   purposes of, 93–96
   replacement, 101–102
   responses to, 29
   self-advocacy questions, 109
   shaping, 92–93
   testing theories, 99–100

Categorizing Goals and Objectives, *see* Activity 8

Certified personnel, *see* Teachers

Classroom Routine, *see* Para Form 5

Classrooms
   arrangements of, 68
   atmosphere of, 104–105

Classrooms—*continued*
changes in, 3
diversity of, 2
inclusion, 4–6
management of, 29
necessity of teamwork in, 21
paraprofessionals in, 9–10
routines in, 23–24
student participation in, 43, 45
Common Components of Daily Routines: Apply to a
Student's Schedule, *see* Para Form 14
Common Components of Daily Routines: Practice with
a Familiar Routine, *see* Para Form 13
Common Components of Daily Routines: Planning
Worksheet, *see* Para Form 15
Communication
behavior and, 88, 90–91, 93–95
maintaining confidentiality, 112–114
reflections in, 22, 29, 36–37
strategies to promote, 30
Communicative intent, 101, 108–109, 109*t*
Communicative Intent of Adult Behaviors, *see* Para
Form 18
Community, 3–5, 6, 29
Community Self-Assessment Checklist, *see* Para Form 1
Confidentiality, 112–118, 117–118, 117*t*
Confidentiality Scenarios, *see* Para Form 25
Creating a Positive Atmosphere, *see* Activity 10
Cues, 77–79, 105, 106*t*
see also Prompts
Curriculum
adaptations to, 70*t*, 79–80
appropriate, 54
literacy and language demands, 61–63, 69, 98–99
multilevel curriculum and instruction, 60–63, 65, 70*t*,
115*t*
overlapping, 60, 63–65, 115*t*
reflections in, 56, 96
responsibilities for, 26–27

Daily routines, 71–76
Daily schedule, 23–24
Data collection, 48, 81, 101, 114
Decision making, 9, 24, 25–26, 59
Delayed responding, 83
Determining Communicative Intent via
Antecedent–Behavior–Consequence (A-B-C), *see*
Para Form 20
Developing the Paraprofessional's Daily Schedule, *see*
Activity 5
Direct verbal prompts, 78*t*, 80*t*, 85*t*

Discussion About the Paraprofessional's Daily Schedule,
see Activity 6
Discussion of Prompting Strategies, *see* Para Form 16
Documenting Spontaneous Incidents, *see* Para Form 24
Effective Utilization of Paraprofessional Support, *see*
Para Form 12
Embedded training, 10
Employment projections, 2
Evaluation, 30–31

Family vision statements, 40–43, 40*f*, 42*f*, 54, 55*f*
Friendships, 34
Full physical prompts, 78*t*, 80*t*, 85*t*

Gestural prompts, 78*t*, 80*t*, 85*t*

IDEA, *see* Individuals with Disabilities Education Act of
1990 (PL 101-476)
see also Individuals with Disabilities Education Act
(IDEA) Amendments of 1997 (PL 107-17);
Individuals with Disabilities Education
Improvement Act (IDEA) of 2004 (PL 108-446)
IEP, *see* Individualized education program
Inclusion
in the classroom, 4–6
demands on the team, 21
effect of personal views, 54
effective use of preteaching, 71
paraprofessionals in, 8–9
reasons for, 55*t*, 56
see also Instruction
Indirect verbal prompts, 78*t*, 80*t*, 85*t*
Individualized education program (IEP)
development of, 29, 42–43, 45–46
example of lesson including, 28*f*
goals of, 66–67
organization of, 114*t*
reflections in, 69
uses of for the paraprofessional, 46
Individualized Education Program Matrix, *see* Para
Form 10
Individuals with Disabilities Education Act (IDEA)
Amendments of 1997 (PL 105-17), 9
Individuals with Disabilities Education Act (IDEA) of
1990 (PL 101-476), 45
Individuals with Disabilities Education Improvement
Act (IDEA) of 2004 (PL 108-446), 7
Instruction
delayed responding, 83
delivery of, 59
goals of, 77

multilevel curriculum, 60–63
Positive behavior support (PBS) strategies, 101
role of team members in, 27–29
specialized, 114–115
specific techniques, 71
strategies for inclusion, 68
support plan, 59, 62*t*, 63
see also Inclusion
Instructional matrix, 81, 82*f*
Instructional prompts, 77–79, 78, 78*t*, 80*t*, 85*t*
Instructional Support Plan, *see* Para Form 17
Interactions, 97–98, 98*t*
see also Peer relationships

Language levels, 61–63, 69
Learning goals, 45–46, 61, 80*f*
Learning outcomes, 61, 65–66, 69
Legal issues, 7, 15, 16*t*
Literacy levels, 61–63, 69, 98–99

Meeting Agenda, *see* Para Form 23
Multilevel curriculum and instruction, 60–63, 65, 70*t*,
    115*t*

Natural prompts, 78*t*, 80*t*, 85*t*
No Child Left Behind (NCLB) Act of 2001 (PL 107-
    110), 7
Note-taking strategies, 64*f*, 67*t*, 83, 84

On-the-job training, 10

Para forms
    Para Form 1 (Community Self-Assessment Checklist), 4
    Para Form 2 (Paraprofessional's Responsibilities), 9
    Para Form 3 (Advocacy Skills for Paraprofessionals:
        Asking for What You Need), 17, 31–32, 104, 114
    Para Form 4 (Welcome Interview worksheet), 21
    Para Form 5 (Classroom Routine worksheet), 23, 24,
        24*f*, 25*f*
    Para Form 6 (Up-Front Issues to Reach Consensus
        On), 26, 29, 30, 31
    Para Form 7 (Problem-Solving on the Fly), 36
    Para Form 8 (Student Profile), 43, 44*f*
    Para Form 9 (Participation in Daily Class Routines), 45
    Para Form 10 (Individualized Education Program
        Matrix), 46, 47*f*, 48, 49
    Para Form 11 (Student Learning Priorities and
        Support), 46, 47*f*, 48, 49, 68
    Para Form 12 (Effective Utilization of
        Paraprofessional Support), 60
    Para Form 13 (Common Components of Daily

    Routines: Practice with a Familiar Routine), 73, 75*f*
    Para Form 14 (Common Components of Daily
        Routines: Apply to a Student's Schedule), 73, 75*f*
    Para Form 15 (Common Components of Daily
        Routines: Planning Worksheet), 73, 76*f*
    Para Form 16 (Discussion of Prompting Strategies),
        79, 80*f*
    Para Form 17 (Instructional Support Plan), 85*f*
    Para Form 18 (Communicative Intent of Adult
        Behaviors), 92
    Para Form 19 (Schedule Analysis), 96
    Para Form 20 (Determining Communicative Intent
        via Antecedent–Behavior–Consequence), 99–100,
        101*f*, 104, 105*f*
    Para Form 21 (Responsibilities Related to
        Encouraging Positive Classroom Behaviors), 104,
        105*f*
    Para Form 22 (Team Communication), 112
    Para Form 23 (Meeting Agenda), 113
    Para Form 24 (Documenting Spontaneous Incidents),
        113
    Para Form 25 (Confidentiality Scenarios), 117
    Para Form 26 (Addressing Confidentiality), 118
Paraprofessionals
    assuming teaching responsibilities, 16–17
    defined, 7–8
    Developing the Paraprofessional's Daily Schedule
        (Activity 5), 24–25
    effects of proximity on students, 32, 33*t*, 50–51
    employment projections, 2
    in individualized education program (IEP) develop-
        ment, 45, 46, 48
    personal views of, 54–55
    reflection activities, 6, 17, 29, 36–37, 57–59, 113
    responsibilities of, 8–9, 22–23, 23, 46, 103
    role clarification, 2, 3, 5–6
    role in communication, 30
    role in delivery of instruction, 27–29
    role in lesson planning, 26–27
    role in preteaching, 71
    role in student evaluation, 30–31
    roles of with students with disabilities, 34–36
    schedules, 27*t*
    self-advocacy questions, 31–32, 67, 76
    teacher support of, 58*f*, 59–60
    training, 7, 10
    see also Adults; Team
Paraprofessional's Responsibilities, *see* Para Form 2
Partial physical prompts, 78*t*, 80*t*, 85*t*
Participation
    active, 73

Participation—*continued*
    in daily routines, 75*f*
    importance of, 43, 45
    increasing, 69, 71
    partial, 76–77
    in shared activities, 61
Participation in Daily Class Routines, *see* Para Form 9
PBS, *see* Positive behavior support
Peer relationships
    effect on behavior, 97–98, 98*t*
    effects of paraprofessional proximity on, 32, 33*t*,
        34–36
    in the family vision, 42
    support for, 45
    see also Interactions
PL 101-476, *see* Individuals with Disabilities Education
        Act (IDEA) of 1990
PL 105-17, *see* Individuals with Disabilities Education
        Act (IDEA) Amendments of 1997
PL 107-110, *see* No Child Left Behind (NCLB) Act of
        2001
PL 108-446, *see* Individuals with Disabilities Education
        Improvement Act (IDEA) of 2004
Positive behavior support (PBS)
    reflections in, 93
    self-advocacy questions, 104
    tenets of, 88–93
    training in, 10
Positive Statements About Kids, *see* Activity 9
Preteaching, 70–71
Problem-Solving on the Fly, *see* Para Form 7
Prompts, 77–79, 78*t*, 80*f*, 85*t*
    see also Cues

Reflection activities
    communication, 36–37
    community, 6
    confidentiality, 113–114, 118
    curriculum, 56
    daily learning, 70
    developing the individualized education program
        (IEP), 69
    inclusion, 96
    paraprofessionals, 113
    positive behavior supports (PBS), 93
    responsibilities, 10
    role clarification, 17, 29, 57–59
    see also activities
Replacement behavior, 101–102

Resources, 62*t*, 68
    see also Tools
Responsibilities
    of the paraprofessional, 8–9, 22–23, 46, 103
    reflection activities in, 10
    of the student, 49, 68
    of the teacher, 2, 9, 23
    of the team, 25–26, 91–92
    using activities to develop, 25*f*
Responsibilities Related to Encouraging Positive
        Classroom Behaviors, *see* Para Form 21
Role clarification
    Activity Debriefing, *see* Activity 2
    applying law to, 7, 15, 16*t*
    of the paraprofessional, 2, 5–6, 8–9
    reflections in, 17, 29, 57–59
    Role Clarification with a Twist, *see* Activity 3
    "Would it be okay?" test, 23, 26, 30, 59
Routines, 45, 71–76
    see also Schedules

Schedule Analysis, *see* Para Form 19
Schedules
    in the classroom, 23–24
    paraprofessionals, 24–25, 26*t*, 27*t*
    picture, 74*f*
    for students with disabilities, 48–49, 67, 73
    see also Routines
Self-advocacy questions
    behavior, 109
    confidentiality, 113–114, 118
    curriculum, 67
    instructional prompts, 79
    for positive behavior support plans (PBS), 104
    questions in assessment, 31–32
    role clarification, 16–17
    routines, 76
    students, 68
    supporting learning priorities, 48
Shared activities, 61, 65
Situation You Know About, *see* Activity 12
Standard assessments, 31
Strategies, *see* Instruction; Positive behavior supports
        (PBS); Support strategies
Student Learning Priorities and Support, *see* Para Form
        11
Student Profile, *see* Para Form 8
Students with disabilities
    accommodations at the high school level, 81–83
    diversity of, 2, 60, 69–70

effects of paraprofessional proximity, 8, 32, 33*t*, 50–51
evaluation of, 30–31
in family vision statement, 41–43
general supports for, 65–66
improving outcomes, 59–60
inclusion, 4–6, 70*t*
independence, 76–77
isolation, 5
learning goals, 45–46, 61
learning schedules, 48–49, 67, 73, 74*f*
need for attention, 94
offering choices to, 106, 107*t*
paraprofessional support of, 34–36, 57–58, 58*f*
preteaching, 70–71
response to cues, 77–79
taking responsibility, 68
team's expectations for, 54–56
Support strategies, 65–66, 75*f*, 80, 115*t*

Teachers
behavior assumptions, 91
interactions with students, 94
modeling, 77
personal views of, 54–55
reflections of, 22
remembering student goals, 115–116, 115*t*
responsibilities of, 2, 3, 9, 23
role in communication, 30
role in delivery of instruction, 27–29
role in instruction, 55
role in lesson planning, 26–27

role in student evaluation, 30–31
supporting paraprofessionals, 58*f*, 59–60
use of power and control, 88, 92–93
see also Adults; Team
Team
assessing needs of, 3–4
communication strategies, 112–113
designing the positive behavior support (PBS) plan,
  102
examining student behaviors, 99–100
expectations for students with disabilities, 54–56
focus on curriculum, 96
focus on outcomes, 66–67
identifying role differences, 14
maintaining confidentiality, 117–118, 117*t*
reflections activities in, 22
responsibilities of, 25–26, 91–92
welcoming new members, 21–22
What Is a Team?, *see* Activity 4
see also Adults; Paraprofessionals; Teachers
Team Communication, *see* Para Form 22
Title I Nonregulatory Guidance, 7, 8
Tools, 62, 81, 82*t*, 83
  see also Resources
Training, 7, 9, 10, 60

Up-Front Issues to Reach Consensus On, *see* Para Form 6

Welcome Interview, *see* Para Form 4
What Is a Team, *see* Activity 4
Who Is Peter?, *see* Activity 7